A Study Of

The Book Of

Ephesians

The Model Of The
New Testament Church

George Runyan

Copyright

A Study of The Book of Ephesians

by George Runyan

Copyright © 2022 by George Runyan

Endorsements

The best thing about Pastor George's writing and teaching on the Book of Ephesians is not the treatment of the subject. The fact is that he has been living as an example of the One New Man before us for decades as a husband, father, pastor, spiritual leader, and a son of God.

Rolland E Slade
Lead pastor Meridian Southern Baptist Church, El Cajon, California
Chairman of the Southern Baptist Convention Executive Committee

George Runyan's study of Paul's letter to the Ephesians is a much-needed resource for the church today. When you read this work, it becomes clear that George has taken great care in his handling of context, culture, and the communication of the original intent of the author. Whether you are a Bible student or a pastor, you will be blessed as you read this work.

Bruce Grecco
Summit Church, San Diego

What a labor of love the author, Dr. George Runyan, has taken through this in-depth study of Ephesians. As a follower of Christ, we must be willing to dig deeply into the writings of the Apostle Paul and the Holy Scriptures. This study will greatly assist you in that endeavor. You will be both enlightened and challenged as you journey through this work!

Richard (Dick) Dungan
Rejoice Ministries International

Dr George Runyan highlights the understanding of the tapestry woven by the Holy Spirit in the Book of Ephesians. We come to the knowledge of the model Church founded on dynamic Apostolic instruction, wisdom, and revelation knowledge. We will experience the pattern and proclamation of actual foundational substance that will grow and influence community culture in our locality and see the maturing of the Church for such a time as this.

This book is a Spirit-led practical commentary with deeply insightful thoughts that will equip and establish you in authentic Apostolic Foundation.

Derek Batte
Dynamic Ministries

Ephesians is perhaps my favorite Book in the Bible because of its powerful revelation about the Kingdom of God and the Church. And George Runyan is the ideal guide to take us through its rich treasures and mysteries. George writes with an authority concerning these great Kingdom principles that can only come from having lived them out and proven them in his own life and ministry over many years. In this book George weds solid biblical exposition with insightful devotional application that can ignite any believer's life. I heartily recommend taking this very profitable journey through the riches of the Book of Ephesians.

Mark Hoffman, Senior Pastor Foothills Christian Church in El Cajon, California

The letter to the church, one church, in Ephesus, written by Paul the apostle, is by far my favorite letter in the Bible. It is a letter, inspired by Holy Spirit, filled with the deepest and most profound New

Testament theology and much practical and highly useful teaching on living a healthy Christian life. I have read and re read, preached and taught from this marvelous letter, which is the crown jewel of Paul's writing.

One would think there were enough books and commentaries on Ephesians…and there certainly are many wonderful works to be commended and worth reading. However, with few exceptions, little of what I have read from others brings the words of Paul to life, words that can be practically applied in a 21st century context like George Runyans' book, *A Study of the Book of Ephesians*. This outstanding work, lived and written from the heart of an apostolic leader, has profound insights, wisdom and practical outworking that will thrill the theologian and inspire the Christian at large. This is an exciting addition to the teaching materials needed to equip this generation to be all the church was designed to be for the Glory of God.

Stan E. DeKoven, Ph.D., D.Litt., MFT
President
Vision International University
Understanding The Mysteries of God Through the Apostle Paul

This intensive and comprehensive book by Apostle George Runyan is amazing! The author's in-depth study of the magnum opus of the apostle Paul, i.e., the Epistle to the Ephesians, unlocks the following essential truths of biblical Christianity: (1) the Christian Life; (2) the Christian Church (Ekklesia); and (3) the Christian Mission.

When an author writes a commentary on Holy Scripture and manages to combine the exegetical, the historical, and the theological dimensions, you know you are in for a wonderful journey into the experience of divine revelation! This book goes way beyond information; it releases revelation. I can tell you it did for me!

Apostle George identifies and clarifies the following which are being restored to the 21st century Church in our day. Let me list them: The Kingdom of God, Soteriology (The doctrine of salvation), The Grace of God, The Mystery of Christ, The New Creation, The Israel of God (Jew and Gentile as the One New Man), The Five Ascension Gift Ministries of Christ, The Spiritual Warfare of the Ekklesia Church, The Seven Spheres of Culture.

I highly recommend this well written and very readable volume. You can use it to enhance your personal study and employ it as a teaching manual to share with others.

Jim Hodges
Founder and President
Federation of Ministers and Churches International

I have studied and taught the book of Ephesians for many years. Dr. George Runyan has made the book of Ephesians come alive to me again in new ways. His many years of study, but more so living, the book of Ephesians, has made his book, *A Study of the Book of Ephesians*, a blessing for many. I know you will thoroughly enjoy it.

Nathan Daniel
Founder of Freedom Through Forgiveness Ministries

Table of Contents

Acknowledgments

Thank you to Paul Runyan for his help with the cover. I am so grateful for the gifts that God has put in your life, and for your willingness to direct it toward the Kingdom of God.

Thank you to John Barry, for all the time that you invest in helping me edit my writings.

Thank you to Dr. Stan Dekoven, for your devoted friendship over many years, and for all the help you have given me in developing my ministry and my anointing for writing.

Thank you to Pastor Bruce Grecco, for going through my manuscript and being the first one to preach through Ephesians using this book.

A special thanks to my wonderful wife, Becky, and all my wonderful children, for their continued support that you give me.

Finally, a grateful thanksgiving to all the pastors in the San Diego region. You are my friends and fellow laborers in equipping the saints for the work of ministry.

Dedication

To All the Shepherds of God's People

THE GREAT SHEPHERD OF THE FLOCK has trusted His sheep's care to multitudes of under-shepherds from the very start of His New Covenant in His broken body and shed blood. As you read *A Study of the Book of Ephesians*, you are reading what Paul, an apostle of Jesus Christ, was writing to the shepherds at Ephesus and throughout the Roman Empire concerning the understanding of what Paul carried for the Lord's church.

I dedicate this Book to all the shepherds I have worked with for over 57 years. I dedicate this book to spiritual fathers I have had, shepherds that God used to lay the foundation in my life upon which to build. I also dedicate this book to the shepherds that are sons to me in the gospel of Christ.

I dedicate this book to servants of God, joint-heirs in Christ, and workers for the "unity of the faith" throughout San Diego. I dedicate this book to the shepherds throughout the San Diego Region to whom I have been joined for over 37 years.

Beginning in 1985, while in prayer, the Holy Spirit spoke a clear word to me, that I was to blow a trumpet and call together shepherds that have been separated from each other through many kinds of divisions in the Lord's body. I asked the Lord how I was to do this? He gave me three keys.

First, tell my shepherds that "I only have one church."

Second, say to my shepherds that the other shepherds are not competitors and enemies. They are your brothers. If the other shepherds are hurting, you're hurting. If they are doing well, then you are doing well.

Third, when my shepherds pray together, I will reveal their hearts to one another.

There is a growing unity to impact the culture for Christ. All over San Diego, some shepherds are joined through prayer and united in purpose to take the Gospel of Christ's Kingdom to the unreached peoples in the San Diego region. The San Diego region is composed of 18 cities. My prayer for many years has been that the shepherds of each of the 18 cities would find each other after Paul's instruction to the shepherds of Ephesus in Acts 20:28,

> *Therefore take heed to yourselves and to all the flock, among which the Holy Spirit has made you overseers, to shepherd the church of God which He purchased with His own blood.*

May grace and peace be multiplied to each one as you read *A Study of the Book of Ephesians*.

George Runyan
Team Leader of City Church Ministries

Foreword

A Study of the Book of Ephesians

DR. GEORGE RUNYAN HAS GIVEN TO US a verse-by-verse study of the book of Ephesians that was circulated among early churches and has been foundational for churches ever since. The Apostle Paul wrote Ephesians around 60 or 61 A.D. while he was in prison awaiting trial. It represents the inspired culmination of his revelation of the mystery of Christ's purpose in and through the church. The church is ordained to be to the praise of His glory on the earth, in spiritual realms and heaven itself. The church will be the masterpiece of His work on earth!

The Church was a mystery hidden for ages until the Lord declared that He would build His church and the gates of hades would not prevail against it. (Matthew 16:18) The Apostle Paul, inspired by the Holy Spirit, further unfolds the mystery of how the Lord will build His victorious church. Therefore, Ephesians is the most vital study for understanding church life, how it was founded, its purpose and its future. The further we journey into this mystery, the more critical the study of Ephesians becomes.

Jesus told His disciples that new wine is not poured into old wineskins. (Luke 5:33-39) Therefore, a new wineskin was required for the new covenant work of Christ and the Holy Spirit. Paul's letter to the Ephesians describes the new wineskin as an unfolding mystery. The church is the new wineskin and we are given the privilege to fellowship and steward this wonderful unfolding mystery. The Apostle Paul unfolds for us how this wineskin is being constructed to reveal the manifold wisdom of God.

Given that the church is a mystery, the apostle uses metaphors to describe it to us: One new man, temple, body, family, bride, warfare

1

and armor. Each metaphor is given to increase the understanding of this mystery for successive generations.

So, we are called to fellowship, share and steward this marvelous mystery of the unfolding purpose of God in and through the church. Therefore, Christ's purpose in and through the church must become our focus.

This is a time of distraction. Too many believers are focused on a multitude of issues that have little to do with what our Lord and the Apostles gave their lives for. A revival, which is so desperately needed, will not only be a revival of power and biblical truth but will be a revival of focus!

The Apostle Paul urges us, even commands us as Jesus did, to be filled with the Holy Spirit. (Acts 1:4-5; Ephesians 5:18-20) The Holy Spirit is our Guide and revealer of God's will. Dr. Runyan is calling us back to the Apostolic foundations of the church, the gifts and calling that construct the church and a renewed focus on the unfolding purpose of God in and through the church. His diligent effort is deserving of our time and study and will help us understand the purpose of God.

I urge you to study Ephesians along with Dr. George Runyan, a longtime friend and a prepared mentor to current and future laborers.

Charles V. Simpson

Introduction

WELCOME IN THE NAME OF THE LORD JESUS! The letter to the Ephesians is a very important document in God's word, the Bible. These pages are intended to clarify and focus biblical truths that are as relevant today as they were when the Apostle Paul penned them in the first century. Allow your heart to be prepared by the Holy Spirit to receive what He wants to impart to you, both in understanding and application. May God help us in the study of the book of Ephesians to receive that which the Spirit has to teach us, not only in academic knowledge of the Word of God, but what the Lord would give to us as an impartation of His Spirit through revelation. The Spirit of God comes and makes alive the Word of God so that it lives in and through us as God's living word.

Father, in Jesus' name, thank you for all you have done for us in Christ. I pray that as we study the word of God, focusing on the book of Ephesians, you would open our hearts and understanding to hear and receive what the Spirit of God wants to convey. Lord, impart to us not only the revelation but the ability to communicate with others as well, to live out Your word in our everyday life. Bless each one that is reading and studying as we labor together in Your word. Help Your servants to be filled with the Holy Spirit and to be able to share precisely and accurately those things that are in your heart. In Jesus' name. Amen.

Background

THE FIRST THING I WANT US TO CONSIDER is the historical background of the Ephesian church. We're not going to spend a lot of time here, but I want you to consider with me Acts 19 and 20. In the process of the development of the New Testament church, Paul the Apostle found himself at Ephesus. This was a very critical and pivotal point in the development of the New Testament church. There are a number of areas in the scripture that are important in understanding the will and the purposes of God for His church on the earth. What the Holy Spirit did in Ephesus is one of those critical biblical areas necessary for our understanding of God's purposes. The book of Acts, chapters 19 and 20, shows us the development of the church at Ephesus. I believe these chapters help us to understand what God wants to accomplish in the church in any given locality on the earth.

Let us examine the first six verses of Acts 19 beginning with verses 1-2:

> *And it happened, while Apollos was at Corinth, that Paul, having passed through the upper regions, came to Ephesus. And finding some disciples he said to them, "Did you receive the Holy Spirit when you believed?"*

> *So they said to him, "We have not so much as heard whether there is a Holy Spirit."*

Please do not misunderstand what is being stated here. (I'm not picking on anybody, nor being critical. It is my desire to stir up our pure minds and to think about some important points.) Have you ever heard someone speak on witnessing using these verses? How do we usually approach a person in trying to determine if they are a believer?

If we think they are a believer, we might ask, "When did you get saved or how did you come to Christ"?

According to the Acts 19 reference, Paul was concerned about their relationship with the Holy Spirit. He simply says to them, "Did you receive the Holy Spirit when you believed?"

Paul is asking a very, very critical question. We are going to build on this question as we go through Ephesians. The Spirit of God is the essence of the Gospel! It is important to realize how, in our evangelical circles, we have misunderstood the emphasis the writers of the New Testament put on the Gospel of the Kingdom. We've made forgiveness of sins and getting to heaven the emphasis, rather than the kingdom of God, which is in the Holy Spirit (ref. Romans 14:17). Well, heaven is God's throne, and certainly, when we die, we want to have the assurance that we're going to be with God, that we're going to be in heaven with the saints and the angelic hosts. I trust we understand that the Bible gives us the truth of our sin condition and that Christ died to redeem us from that condition. The cross makes it possible for us to enter the kingdom of God. The kingdom is about a New Creation that the Holy Spirit is bringing forth on the earth. God has sent His Holy Spirit from heaven to earth to indwell believers so that heaven can dwell in us and there can be a demonstration on the earth of the lordship of our God through Christ in the power of His indwelling Spirit.

The essence of the Gospel is bringing an individual to an encounter with the Holy Spirit because the Holy Spirit is the one who convicts of sin. The Holy Spirit is the one who empowers us to live unto righteousness. It is the Holy Spirit who gives us revelation of Christ as Lord and Savior. He is the one who gives understanding to a person. It is the Holy Spirit who is the very Spirit of God. Romans 8:9 says:

> *But you are not in the flesh but in the Spirit, if indeed the Spirit of God dwells in you. Now if anyone does not have the Spirit of Christ, he is not His.*

You belong to Jesus by receiving the Holy Spirit, who is God's assurance of the completed work. Ephesians 1:13 states: "In Him you also trusted, after you heard the word of truth, the gospel of your salvation; in whom also, having believed, you were sealed with the Holy Spirit of promise." Now, I understand that today we have many theological thoughts about the Holy Spirit. However, we're going to look to Paul and his relationship to the Ephesian church and what he tells them about the Holy Spirit—not only what he tells them but how the Spirit demonstrated His presence in the church at Ephesus.

Paul's essential question of these disciples in Ephesus was:

"Did you receive the Holy Spirit when you believed?"

Their answer was: "We have not so much as heard whether there is a Holy Spirit."

Paul certainly had an interesting dialog with these disciples. Paul saw them as believers, but they hadn't heard of the Holy Spirit. Notice the next verse.

And he said to them, "Into what then were you baptized?

So they said, "Into John's baptism."

An important thing must be remembered in this conversation. Paul was asking these disciples, "What was your purpose of baptism?" You see, that's why he thought they were believers, because they had been baptized. Most likely, Paul had heard a report from Apollos because Apollos had been there earlier. Apollos was an evangelist who was baptizing people (see Acts 18:24-25). The Bible indicates that Apollos was lacking in understanding according to Acts 18:26. Aquila and Priscilla took Apollos aside and privately instructed him more accurately in the Word of God. He was an eloquent preacher but limited in his understanding of the complete revelation of Christ. This presents an interesting point: One can be an eloquent preacher and still be limited in their understanding. There are many eloquent people around who have a very limited perspective of the eternal purpose of God. They are eloquent but they lack a full understanding of God's plan and purposes. That was the problem that Paul encountered at Ephesus.

In answering Paul, saying it was John's baptism, it was clear that these believers were looking for the coming Messiah. They were baptized in water and received from God a preparation for Messiah's coming. They had not entered into what Messiah had accomplished in His atoning work on the cross. They were like forerunners, living in the hope of the coming kingdom. When Paul arrived, he presented to them the essence of the gospel, which is the Holy Spirit.

The story continued to unfold in verse 4:

> *Then Paul said," John indeed baptized with a baptism of repentance, saying to the people that they should believe on Him who would come after him, that is, on Christ Jesus."*

This included all those who were baptized with John's baptism, and even those who were baptized by the disciples. They were baptizing people, preparing them and readying them for the receiving of the Holy Spirit. The Messiah, as we're going to read in Ephesians, went to the grave and to hades with our sins. He was raised from the dead and God exalted him by seating Him next to Himself. Father God gave Him the promise that had been made to Him. The Holy Spirit was poured out upon all those who would believe on Him. The receiving of the Holy Spirit is the receiving of the very nature of Christ.

In verse 5, we read:

> *When they heard this, they were baptized in the name of the Lord Jesus.*

They had been baptized previously, looking forward to Messiah's reign. Now they were baptized in the name of the Lord Jesus. Why? The Bible tells us that after the resurrection and the ascension, God gave Jesus a name above every name. Baptism is not effective if we're baptized in the name of the church. Some churches actually practice this kind of baptism for one to be part of that church group, baptized in their particular persuasion rather than into Christ. That's not what the Bible is teaching us. The Bible says that our baptism has nothing to do with a title or a denominational name, or lack of such. It has to do with the name of Jesus. Verse 6, says,

> *And when Paul had laid hands on them, the Holy Spirit came upon them, and they spoke with tongues and prophesied.*

They were obedient, and they were baptized with a purpose. The first purpose was repentance and preparation. The second purpose was to receive the Holy Spirit. And after an encounter with the Holy Spirit, there were supernatural manifestations—a supernatural experience.

Let's draw a contrast here. I'm trying to prepare our thinking as we look deeper into the book of Ephesians. Down through church history, men have taught about the Holy Spirit, but it's similar to the way we present salvation. Believe it and hope it's all going to work out in the end. We'll show people scripture, and because they did what the scripture says we will have faith that God will honor their obedience by receiving them in heaven. There's a place for that practice, but I want to say that God is a God of the present, He's not a god that calls us to blind faith. Many say, "I did what the Bible says, I confessed Jesus and I opened my heart to receive Him. I hope I'm going to heaven. I hope I'm going to be saved. I hope everything is going to be ok." No, God wants to meet us in the now. God wants us to have an encounter with Him. I want to encourage the reader that, as we present Christ to people or we understand these things, we can have confidence to lead them into a supernatural experience in God. Not a head trip, not just believing a theology, but a life-changing encounter with the living God. That's what it's about, having an encounter with God, not once, but every day. This truth is made exceedingly clear in the book of Ephesians, to be seen as we go through this epistle. The Spirit of God has come to indwell us, to live inside of us, to possess us, and to reveal

Christ, not only to us, but through us to a world needing God's grace and mercy.

As we continue to look at the book of Acts, we see the development of the church in this city. This was a church planted by Paul, a church that began to affect the culture in Ephesus. Paul goes to the synagogue because his first assignment was to go to the Jews, his own people. He spent 3 months preaching and teaching, interacting with the Jews in the synagogue. Acts 19:8, "And he went into the synagogue, and spoke boldly for the space of three months, disputing and persuading the things concerning the kingdom of God." He is not disputing a theology, but the reality of the resurrected Christ who is revealed through the Holy Spirit convicting of sin and Jesus' Lordship.

Let this thought take root. I wrote of the essence of the gospel. I said, it is the receiving of the Holy Spirit. The message is about the kingdom and not the church. The church is the vehicle for extending the kingdom, but the church is not the kingdom. Through the church and through what God has ordained in the preaching of the Word of God, the message is expressed, conviction comes through the power of the Holy Spirit and people are added to the church. They enter the kingdom and come face to face with lordship, the rule and the reign of Messiah, the Lord Jesus Christ. That's what our message is about, bringing people, not only to salvation and forgiveness so they can go to heaven, but to encounter and submit to Christ's Lordship through the power of the Holy Spirit.

Paul had many problems as he presented this gospel in the synagogue because the message begins to confront religious people that were hardened in their hearts, who refused to believe. They began to speak evil of That Way. Now in the first century, the early church was known as The Way or That Way. If you were talking about the church, you wouldn't say the church over here or over there. In the early days of the church, the world would speak of That Way. Why? Because the message was pointing somewhere, it had a direction it pointed people toward. It wasn't like all the other religions, worshiping all these other gods. There was a direction to the message with singleness of purpose. They were going somewhere, the rule and reign of God on the earth through His Son, Jesus, manifested in the Holy Spirit in believers' lives. That Way was pointing somewhere. I must ask this question of the reader. Does our life point somewhere? When people touch us, are they influenced by us? Do people perceive where we are going? They might reject where we're going, but do they understand we're going somewhere?

The book of Acts goes on to say that Paul departed from the synagogue and separated with the disciples those that believed, those that were trusting Christ and submitting to Paul. Notice the word disciples; these are not church-goers. These weren't people going to a Sunday morning meeting to receive a little inspiration to get them through the week. These were learners! I would guess, because you're reading this book, you are a disciple too. You're a learner. Those that attend our School of Ministry in San Diego take their time and spend their money and say, "I want to be instructed, I want to learn." That is what God desires, learners. He desires those who will come under instruction and begin to receive the teaching, and then the learner becomes the teacher. They become those that are able to communicate the plan and the purpose of God to others. That is what God desires. He is not looking for a bunch of people that warm pews or merely occupy chairs on a Sunday morning, get a little inspiration, go home and watch football. That is not what God has in His mind. He is looking for disciples, disciplined people, people that are in the Word, people that are speaking the mind of God, trying to find out what scripture is all about, and then making application in their life and helping others.

Paul takes the disciples out of the synagogue system and continues to instruct them. He *"separated the disciples, disputing daily in the school of one Tyrannus."* Then, more disciples were added to the Lord's work. The synagogue couldn't hold what God was about to do. I've got news for us. Our church buildings aren't going to be able to hold what God wants to do. In fact, and please don't misunderstand what I'm going to say here, but it concerns me when I see congregations involved with million-dollar projects relating to church buildings–could it be that our vision is really too small? God wants to do more than what any building that has been built in our city can hold. I'm not saying we're not supposed to have buildings. I'm simply saying that we need to put things into perspective. The buildings serve a certain purpose, but if we're building to 2,000, guess what? It's not big enough! Churches grow, and then level off. They don't go past a certain point because their vision is too small. God is planning for increase, and our buildings aren't going to be able to hold what God is getting ready to do. This was certainly true of the church at Ephesus.

The disciples were multiplying, so Paul went to a school called Tyrannus, and he rented it. "And this continued by the space of two years." So for 2 years, the apostle spent his days in a school of ministry, instructing and teaching the disciples. People were being added to the church every day; it was growing. It was a holy temple growing in the Lord, increasing in its size as Paul was instructing. Let's review what happened: "So that all they which dwelt in Asia heard the word of the Lord Jesus, both Jews and Greeks." When it says Asia, it's talking about Asia Minor. It's not talking about China and the whole of Asia. It's talking about Asia Minor where the seven churches of Revelation were located. So, all of Asia Minor heard the word of the Lord because of what God did at Ephesus because of teaching and training. All this happened when they separated out of the synagogue system and into a larger vision, into a larger purpose, into an instruction that could contain the growth. They did not just go home after instruction, but they went out and preached the kingdom everywhere.

The Word of God and the Spirit of God will lead us out to a lost world if we have heard accurately. We've got to do something about this Gospel of the Kingdom. There's a mandate that comes with the Gospel. If one understands what is stated here and believes the Gospel, one must act upon it. That action will require the power of the Holy Spirit to fulfill the mandate. When the word is taught and one is open to the Holy Spirit we are required to act upon the word. If we fail to act, we have not truly heard nor learned. We must find out individually where God is leading us and how he wants to use us. God could move us into a ministry office, but it is also possible that he may use us in a secular job, or it might be in our neighborhood, with our family and possibly in all of these. The point is, we are responsible for what we have learned and received. We can't say, "Oh, wasn't that wonderful, boy, that blessed me." We must respond to the Gospel of the Kingdom in action and demonstration to glorify God.

We see something else that began while Paul was at Ephesus. God did special miracles by the hands of Paul. Sweatbands were brought to the sick, and people got healed of diseases and delivered from evil spirits. Notice what happened. Out of the proclamation of the Word of God, the church at Ephesus begins to grow and influence the culture in the city. It's not just teaching and preaching, but the supernatural work of the Holy Spirit that produces church life and growth.

Something happens when we come into the purposes of God. When we begin to do it God's way, when we allow the Holy Spirit access, control and leadership, not bound by systems, but separated to God's purpose, something begins to happen in the miraculous. The Christian religion is no different than any other religion if you remove the miraculous. It's just a lot of good philosophy and natural thinking. It might make one feel good about oneself. It is not about feeling good about oneself, though that will come. In the Holy Spirit, we have righteousness, peace and joy, all part of the package, but it's not about feeling good about yourself. It's about obeying God. That's what Paul was doing, obeying God. Further, the disciples were also obeying God. The Lord then released the supernatural; the power of God was manifest. Look at Acts 19:17-18 KJV, "And this was known to all the Jews and Greeks also dwelling at Ephesus; and fear fell on them all, and the name of the Lord Jesus was magnified. And many that believed came, and confessed, and showed their deeds."

In fact, the person and power of God manifested so much, it even affected the economy of the city. The economy was built on the worship of false gods through the purchasing of idols. Our economy also focuses on false gods. How about Hollywood? Is that a false god? Humanism and materialism are the false gods of our age. People are worshipping every day, in front of the TV set, the gods of this world. We don't think of it that way, but that's exactly what's happening in the city of Ephesus. Imagine a move of the Spirit of God-like they had at Ephesus in your city. People begin to deal with their videos and some of their computer stuff and did what they did at Ephesus, bringing it to the streets and burning it in a bonfire. There would be incredible upheaval. That's exactly what happened at Ephesus. The silver makers, the makers of the statues, became enraged because they were losing business badly. The church was growing and the people were worshipping Jesus, not Diana. Do you think God could do that today? He is looking for participants, for people who will participate with him like those at Ephesus.

The merchants became very stirred up and the church assembly was taken to the market place becoming the Ekklesia or church of God. We understand the word Ekklesia is the Greek word for assembly. It's a word that was assigned to the church because God's people assembled. The word church was first used by the world before it became what we know it as today. Any assembly was known as an Ekklesia. The clerk or mayor of the city announces that the people had gathered unlawfully in this assembly. No one gave permission to assemble like this. He got involved not on an emotional level, but he dealt with the leaders behind the riot. He confronted the people and he dismissed the illegal ekklesia or church. He dismissed the crowd. We're not talking about the church of the Lord. The Bible says there was such a move of God, and they were under such conviction that they destroyed all of the occult books they owned. Would to God that that would happen again in our cities.

The Bible doesn't give us great detail, but we read in other places that Paul had sent his deputy, Timothy, to Ephesus. As the church emerged there was a need for structure and order. Elders were set in to oversee the early churches. These were men who had the gifting and ability of God to shepherd and give oversight to God's people. It's interesting as we look at the church in Ephesus; it wasn't a singular person who was a shepherd. The Bible doesn't represent a hierarchy, but rather a plural leadership in Ephesus. It speaks about a plurality of leaders. Different words are used that carry similar meanings in the original language, words such as elders, bishops, or overseers. The Bible pictures team ministry as opposed to one-man leadership.

The word pastor as it relates to shepherding God's people is used most frequently today and has been for many years. The word is only found one time in scripture and that is in Ephesians chapter four. The better understanding is bishop or overseer. There were overseers that were raised up and they worked together to give oversight and care to the whole church in a city setting. It wasn't about this group meeting in this house or that house. The early believers understood the church, local, in relationship to localities or the church of a city. As Paul writes to the church at Ephesus, he doesn't write to the churches of Ephesus, he writes to the Church at Ephesus. God sees it differently than we do. In El Cajon, where I am involved with pastors, God doesn't see a bunch of churches, He sees His Church, born of the Spirit of God, under the oversight and care of leadership. God's trying to get the leaders together to cooperate and receive a vision of a larger dimension of what God wants to do in a locality. Ephesus gives to us that picture; it gives to us a model of church life.

In Acts 20, Paul passes by Ephesus, and he sends for the elders of Ephesus to come and meet him in Miletus. Notice the language Luke uses in Acts 20:17, "He sent to Ephesus, and called the elders of the church." Not churches, but the church. There was only one church in the city. Paul gives the elders their final instructions for the care of God's flock.

"Therefore take heed to yourselves and to all the flock, among which the Holy Spirit has made you overseers, to shepherd the church of God which He purchased with His own blood."

Acts 20:28

These elders were accountable to one another, had the responsibility to feed the flock and to keep in mind that the flock is His flock, bought with His blood.

In conclusion: Ephesus is a model church, begun evangelistically, with an inadequate foundation, but re-established by the apostle Paul who functioned as a wise, master builder. The church grew, under dynamic apostolic instruction, deep fellowship and signs and wonders. After two years, elders, overseers emerged. Asia Minor received the gospel and our pattern for church planting and developing emerged. (*Supernatural Architecture Building the Church in the 21st Century*, Dr. Stan DeKoven.)

Join me now as we ask the Holy Spirit to teach us from God's Word and help to ground each of us in the truth as we seek to follow our Lord in our daily walk! You may or may not be familiar with Paul's Letter to the Ephesians, but I can guarantee that you will not be disappointed as you are renewed in the book of Ephesians, or you are exploring it for the first time.

Ephesians is addressed to a group of believers who are rich beyond measure in Jesus Christ, yet living as beggars, and only because they are ignorant of their wealth, not unlike many today.

In chapters one through three, Paul describes what God has provided and reserved in heaven for every believer. Like a bank account, one must withdraw what has been deposited in order to invest and produce growth. Consider how chapters one through three reveal the content of what belongs to believers, such things as: adoption, acceptance, redemption, forgiveness, wisdom, inheritance, the seal of the Holy Spirit, life, grace and citizenship. Paul's summary is: "Every spiritual blessing." These spiritual blessings will be highlighted and discussed throughout our study.

In chapters four through six, as believers we learn of our spiritual walk rooted in His spiritual wealth. In Ephesians 2:10 Paul says "For we are His workmanship created in Christ Jesus for good works." We are to walk in those good works. We were created to walk in good works as His life is received and operates in and through us.

In chapter six we learn that it is a battle to walk out His Kingdom purposes because we are wrestling against spiritual forces.

Although Paul's letter is titled *Ephesians*, it is meant to be a circular letter. In other words, the truths contained here are eternal and meant for all believers to know and understand so that they might fulfill God's will lived out in His new creation of the Spirit. That creation is "one new man" on the earth fulfilling God's will and living out of God's life.

Chapter 1

Ephesians 1:1-2

Paul, an apostle of Jesus Christ by the will of God, to the saints who are in Ephesus, and faithful in Christ Jesus: Grace to you and peace from God our Father and the Lord Jesus Christ.

Unfolding The Mystery

In verse 1, Paul establishes his identity as "an apostle of Jesus Christ by the will of God." The term *apostle* was not a title but a gift from the Chief Apostle: The Lord Jesus Christ, who was sent from God. Paul was sent by Christ Jesus according to God's will. This is evident as one studies the book of Acts and Paul's epistles to our Lord's church. Not only is an apostle a sent one, but he also lays the foundation for the church Christ is building. He is a master builder, an architect, one who has the plans.

In today's spiritual atmosphere, there are many who call themselves apostles. As I work with leaders across denominational lines, I find that very few understand what an apostle truly is called to do. He is not necessarily leading a big church or has a large network of churches, although he could have and do these things. Yet a true apostle touches the church. He helps restore the church to the doctrine of those first apostles, not the reformers of the reformation but the apostles that the Father gave to Jesus. He is gifted to be prophetic, he is gifted to evangelize, he is gifted to shepherd, and he is gifted to teach. He is a foundation person, a servant, not a top-down CEO.

We will look deeper into the subject of apostles in the second and fourth chapters of Ephesians. For now, please consider with me that

Paul and the other apostles of the Lord were the ones given the wisdom of God to unfold what the Bible calls the mysteries hidden in the Old Testament. Through the wisdom given to them by the Holy Spirit, they laid the foundation of the Lord's true apostolic church. Those apostles carried the Lord's design for the church He wanted to be built. It was never about those men God had chosen; it was about the Lord's Kingdom purposes. Today, one of the ways we can judge true apostolic ministry is by discerning whether the message and the messenger are fully focused on Christ rather than the messenger or his ministry. Apostolic gifting is needed today to help God's people come back to what the Apostles of the Lamb, including Paul, understood to be God's will and purpose. Much has been lost in 2000 years of church history, but the Lord is moving by His Spirit to restore and establish His holy apostolic church on the earth.

As we will see in going through this study, the book of Ephesians is critical in helping us refocus on the Lord's plans. The letter to the Ephesian Christians is essential to grounding us in biblical truths that will help us live out the adventure of walking with Christ in the twenty-first century.

Paul is writing to the saints in Ephesus, which he calls "faithful in Christ Jesus." What would Paul say if he was writing personally to us? Do we fit the classification of saints? Consider the word Paul uses with the word *saints*: *faithful*. I believe this to be the best definition of a saint: one who is faithful!

Revelation 2:2-3 holds keys to understanding Paul's use of the word *faithful*. Jesus says to these Ephesian believers:

> *I know your works, your labor, your patience, and that you cannot bear those who are evil. And you have tested those who say they are apostles and are not, and have found them liars: and you have persevered and have patience, and have labored for My name's sake and have not become weary.*

Grace and Peace

Ephesians 1:2, says:

> *Grace to you and peace from God our Father and the*
> *Lord Jesus Christ.*

This is known as The Apostolic Greeting. God's will for His children is grace and peace. An apostolic foundation is the grace of God being extended to all who will receive…not just once but continually. Grace is a flow of God's love to His people.

Some call grace "unmerited favor." It is like being adorned with precious jewels. As saints, we are expected to wear the grace of God by being gracious toward all, even those who have not received God's grace. We are to be carriers of His grace. Saints of God are called to be the demonstration of God's grace to a lost and perishing world. Grace is about the life of Christ in us, lived out through the power of the Holy Spirit. That means that grace is the means to holiness and living a holy life.

The result of grace is peace. Note Romans 5:1-2:

> *Therefore, having been justified by faith, we have*
> *peace with God through our Lord Jesus Christ,*
> *through whom we have access by faith into this grace*
> *in which we stand, and rejoice in hope of the glory of*
> *God.*

Faith, grace, and peace all work together. They are given by God our Father and the Lord Jesus Christ in love through the power of the Holy Spirit.

Ephesians 1:3-6

Blessed be the God and Father of our Lord Jesus Christ, who has blessed us with every spiritual blessing in the heavenly places in Christ, just as He chose us in Him before the foundation of the world, that we should be holy and without blame before Him in love, having predestined us to adoption as sons by Jesus Christ to Himself, according to the good pleasure of His will, to the praise of the glory of His grace, by which He made us accepted in the Beloved.

Discovering Our Part

As we study this great book, understand we are on a great adventure in discovering God's plan for developing His church on the earth. The Holy Spirit continues to be poured out on His body so we can fulfill the calling and mandate given by Jesus, first to His apostles in the first century and then to us. That calling and mandate continue today. Each believer has a part. One of our challenges is to discover our part in the great adventure for which our Lord has called us.

Paul was sent by God and He communicates grace and peace to these saints. Paul's first order is to bless God. Jesus taught us the pattern for prayer in Matthew 6:9-13

Our Father in heaven,
Hallowed be Your name.
Your kingdom come.
Your will be done
On earth as it is in heaven.
Give us this day our daily bread.
And forgive us our debts,
As we forgive our debtors.
And do not lead us into temptation,
But deliver us from the evil one.

22

For Yours is the kingdom and the power
And the glory forever.
Amen.

Notice: "Our Father in heaven," followed by "hallowed be Your name." In these verses, Paul underscores that God is the Father of our Lord Jesus Christ.

Jesus, the man, has been raised from the dead. Jesus, who is the promised seed of the women in Genesis 3:15.

And I will put enmity
Between you and the woman,
And between your seed and her Seed;
He shall bruise your head,
And you shall bruise His heel."

Abraham rejoiced to see Jesus' day (see John 8:56) because He is the seed promised to Abraham. Jesus, the son of David, and the promised heir of David's throne was also the Son of God (see 2 Samuel 7). A man is now seated in heaven for us.

Seeing then that we have a great High Priest who has passed through the heavens, Jesus the Son of God, let us hold fast our confession. For we do not have a High Priest who cannot sympathize with our weaknesses, but was in all points tempted as we are, yet without sin. Let us therefore come boldly to the throne of grace that we may obtain mercy and find grace to help in time of need.

Hebrews 4:14-16

In Ephesians 1:3 we read that the Father has blessed us—His sons and daughters—with every spiritual blessing in heavenly places in Christ. Here is seen the heavenly bank account. These spiritual blessings are deposited in heavenly places, and they are there because Christ is there.

Here is how Paul expresses this:

I have been crucified with Christ; it is no longer I who live, but Christ lives in me; and the life which I now live in the flesh I live by faith in the Son of God, who loved me and gave Himself for me.

Galatians 2:20

Paul, in Ephesians 5, instructs the believer when he says:

Therefore be imitators of God as dear children. And walk in love, as Christ also has loved us and given Himself for us, an offering and a sacrifice to God for a sweet-smelling aroma.

Ephesians 5:1-2

What are those spiritual blessings? Some of those blessings are:

1. adoption into God's family
2. acceptance, redemption
3. forgiveness
4. wisdom
5. inheritance
6. life in Christ
7. grace
8. citizenship

All this is sealed with the Holy Spirit of promise. Consider this question: Are you laying hold of all that belongs to you?

Just as He chose us in Him before the foundation of the world, that we should be holy and without blame before Him in love,

Ephesians 1:4

An important matter we must understand is that we are *chosen.* The plan of God was born in God's heart before the foundation of the world. Our all-knowing heavenly Father knew man would fall and

24

Satan would rule on the earth, so God planned to provide redemption for His creation man. God Himself would become the sacrifice for His creation man who was made a little lower than the angels (ref. Hebrews 2:7). God would raise man from the dead and seat him in the heavenly places to reign with God forever. Jesus Christ is that first man to sit at the Father's right hand.

In Ephesians 1:5, God predetermined that His redeemed people would be holy and without blame before Him in love. What was predetermined? It was a redeemed people made holy, without blame, in love. I was not predetermined up against some who were not included. No! What was predetermined was a people—a holy covenant people who are blameless in love! This is how God our Father wants us to see ourselves in the context of a new creation, a new man, and God's holy people!

Predestination can be a confusing subject when interpreted within the context of the Protestant Reformation. Some believe that our salvation is determined by our free will, while others believe that God predetermined who is saved and who is not. This subject has divided the Lord's church for centuries.

Predestination is about God's predetermined plan to legally make it possible for us to be adopted into the family of God as sons. In Hebrew culture, it was the eldest son who had the right to the inheritance. (Remember Jacob and Esau.) Well, God predetermined the adoption of sons through Jesus Christ to Himself. These are those who were redeemed (purchased) out of the slavery of sin and the kingdom of darkness. We see how Paul expressed the transaction in Colossians 1:13 when he said, "He has delivered us from the power of darkness and translated us into the kingdom of the Son of His love."

In Ephesians 1:5, this was stated as: "According to the good pleasure of His will." God chose us just because He wanted to. It was His pleasure to make mankind the focus of that pleasure. His will! He knew from the beginning what He would do.

Peter says,

> *But, beloved, do not forget this one thing, that with the Lord one day is as a thousand years, and a thousand years as one day. The Lord is not slack concerning His promise, as some count slackness, but is longsuffering toward us, not willing that any should perish but that all should come to repentance.*
>
> *But the day of the Lord will come as a thief in the night, in which the heavens will pass away with a great noise, and the elements will melt with fervent heat; both the earth and the works that are in it will be burned up.*
>
> 2 Peter 3:8-10

Note from this verse that our will is involved. We choose whether to receive God's grace and enter into life or to reject His grace and perish. Our choice! God predetermined a way to life eternal through the adoption as sons in His kingdom.

Consider Ephesians 1:6.

> *To the praise of the glory of His grace, by which He made us accepted in the Beloved.*

All that our heavenly Father has done is to the praise of the glory of His grace. Grace is in the nature of God. Grace does not stand alone as simply theological but is the expression of God's good pleasure activated by His will! By grace He made us accepted in the Beloved! By grace through faith our salvation has come! Acceptance is what we have been offered and how we stand complete in His favor! Not rejected but accepted.

Quit condemning yourself! Quit entertaining rejection! Quit believing the lies of the devil! Quit letting your imaginations strip you of God's measureless grace, acceptance and love. If you have trusted Jesus to have done the work of redemption, then receive His guarantee of acceptance in the Beloved.

Remember the old hymn:

Stand Up Stand Up for Jesus
Ye soldiers of the cross
Lift high His royal banner
It must not suffer loss,
From victory unto victory
His Army shall He shall lead
Until every foe is vanquished
And Christ is Lord indeed.

George Duffield, Jr., 1858

If you have trusted Christ but are still wrestling with your self-acceptance and God's acceptance of you, let this be your time of freedom. Reject every lie of the enemy and receive His acceptance through His grace and love. Receive by faith all that Jesus has done for you. Receive the infilling of His Holy Spirit right now in order to be empowered to live in His victory over sin, death and the enemy!

Ephesians 1:7-14

In Him we have redemption through His blood, the forgiveness of sins, according to the riches of His grace which He made to abound toward us in all wisdom and prudence, having made known to us the mystery of His will, according to His good pleasure which He purposed in Himself, that in the dispensation of the fullness of the times He might gather together in one all things in Christ, both which are in heaven and which are on earth—in Him. In Him also we have obtained an inheritance, being predestined according to the purpose of Him who works all things according to the counsel of His will, that we who first trusted in Christ should be to the praise of His glory.

In Him you also trusted, after you heard the word of truth, the gospel of your salvation; in whom also, having believed, you were sealed with the Holy Spirit of promise, 14 who is the guarantee of our inheritance until the redemption of the purchased possession, to the praise of His glory.

Our Redemption

Notice that verse 7 begins with "In Him." Paul said in verse 6, "He made us accepted in the beloved." We are not just accepted, but that acceptance is in Him, that is Jesus who is the "Author and finisher of our faith" (Hebrews 12:2). It is what Jesus was teaching His disciples when He said, "enter through the narrow gate" (Luke 13:24). Jesus is that gate (or door) to life eternal. There is no wiggle room. Everything God the Father does is in Christ Jesus His Son! Not our works, nor our organized church affiliation and not our natural talents or abilities. He sees us in Him. He receives us in Him and He uses us because Jesus already fulfilled the work of God. "My Father has been working until now, and I have been working" (John 5:17).

In Jesus we have redemption. It is because of Jesus that we have been purchased, fully belonging to Him and the Father. We are His purchased possession. This is the true meaning of redemption. We are His purchased redemptive sons and daughters. We have been bought with the blood of Christ—the blood of God's sinless sacrifice given for the world by eternal love. This is what made forgiveness possible! "Forgiveness of sins, according to the riches of His grace." This is the first major deposit into our heavenly bank account. We are forgiven, and it is a powerful reality that can strengthen us every day. Our Father loves us with a powerful life-changing love of His grace. The favor of God is upon me! Let this understanding work into your heart and soul!

Verse 8: "He made to abound toward us." God's grace was made to abound toward every believer, that is, everyone who puts their trust in God's dear Son by receiving His forgiveness and His new creation life in the Holy Spirit! That grace is received not just once, but again and again in the myriad ways that He favors His children.

Verse 9: Paul says that what God did was both "In all wisdom and prudence." The cross was the wisdom of God

> *But to those who are called, both Jews and Greeks, Christ the power of God and the wisdom of God.*
>
> 1 Corinthians 1:24

> *But of Him you are in Christ Jesus, who became for us wisdom from God—and righteousness and sanctification and redemption—that as it is written He who glories, let him glory in the Lord.*
>
> 1 Corinthians 1:30-31

It was His good judgment to make known to each believer "the mystery of His will."

What Is That Mystery?

Let's understand that within the mystery was "His good pleasure." God just wanted to lavish His creation man with His absolute love. His love is way beyond our ability to comprehend, but by faith we can receive His love and experience His love and even pass His love on to others through the work of His Spirit in us. He did all this by purposing it in Himself. Don't try to figure it out, because you can't. Just receive His grace, receive His love, and receive His acceptance, and then give it away to others through your manner of living!

The Mystery Was for A Certain Time!

Verse 10:

> *That in the dispensation of the fullness of the times He might gather together in one all things in Christ, both which are in heaven and which are on earth—in Him.*

Paul expressed it this way to the Galatians:

> *But when the fullness of the time had come, God sent forth His Son, born of a woman, born under the law, to redeem those who were under the law, that we might receive the adoption as sons.*

> Galatians 4:4-5

The fullness of time, or the day of the Lord, is not the end of the world, but it was the end of an age—the age of Moses, the age of the Law as a means of righteousness.

The present age belongs to Christ and His followers. It is the age of the Spirit (see Joel 2:28-32), the age of a whole new creation on the earth (see Isaiah 43:19 and 2 Corinthians 5:17). This is the work of the Holy Spirit, as we will see, who has sealed us. He was given to us as the down payment of our future in Christ, our eternal King.

The first fourteen verses in Ephesians 1 are one continuous thought from Paul. Verse 10 defines the time.

> *That in the dispensation of the fullness of the times He might gather together in one all things in Christ, both which are in heaven and which are on earth—in Him. In Him also we have obtained an inheritance, being predestined according to the purpose of Him who works all things according to the counsel of His will, that we who first trusted in Christ should be to the praise of His glory. In Him you also trusted, after you heard the word of truth, the gospel of your salvation; in whom also, having believed, you were sealed with the Holy Spirit of promise, who is the guarantee of our inheritance until the redemption of the purchased possession, to the praise of His glory.*

> Ephesians 1:10-14

The "dispensation of the fullness of times" means: "a system of order, government, or organization of a nation, community, etc., especially as existing at a particular time. Synonyms, order, scheme, plan, arrangement and organization."

God's dispensation plans revolve around Christ and His kingdom! It includes heaven and earth. See Hebrews 12 for a New Testament view of the throne of Christ presently.

Eight Important Points

1. *He might gather together in one all things in Christ...*

Man has his plans, whether speaking personally, culturally or of nations. Man makes his plans, but God is working out His plan and His plan trumps the plans of man. God's total plan is in Christ and nothing else. This is why it is important to understand the biblical

31

revelation that our life is in Christ and His life dwells in us through His Holy Spirit.

2. *Both which are in heaven and earth—in Him.*

   Paul brings clarity to this point in his discussion of the catching away in 1 Corinthians 15:50-58.

3. *In Him also we have obtained an inheritance, being predestined according to the purpose of Him who works all things according to the counsel of His will...*

   The inheritance which Paul is addressing is directly related to reigning with Christ. When did that reign begin? When one is born again of Christ's Holy Spirit. Consider Romans 8:29, "For whom He foreknew, He also predestinated to be conformed to the image of His Son, that He might be the firstborn among many brethren."

   Also consider Romans 5:17, "For if by the transgression of one man, death reigned through the one, much more those who receive the abundance of grace and of the gift of righteousness will reign in life through the One, Jesus Christ."

4. *That we who first trusted Christ are to the praise of His glory...*

   In the first century, today and throughout eternity those first believers have led the way for each of us!

5. *In Him you also trusted, after you heard the word of truth, the gospel of your salvation;*

   What is that *word of truth*? Paul expresses it this way in Galatians 3:1.

   > *O foolish Galatians! Who has bewitched you that you should not obey the truth, before whose eyes Jesus Christ was clearly portrayed among you as crucified?*

   Again in 1 Corinthians 15:1-8.

Moreover, brethren, I declare to you the gospel which I preached to you, which also you received and in which you stand, by which also you are saved, if you hold fast that word which I preached to you —unless you believed in vain. For I delivered to you first of all that which I also received: that Christ died for our sins according to the Scriptures, and that He was buried, and that He rose again the third day according to the Scriptures, and that He was seen by Cephas, then by the twelve. After that He was seen by over five hundred brethren at once, of whom the greater part remain to the present, but some have fallen asleep. After that He was seen by James, then by all the apostles. Then last of all He was seen by me also, as by one born out of due time.

6. Because of belief, we were sealed with the Holy Spirit of promise verse 13, the Holy Spirit is given. He is not just a theology or a mystical being; He is the Spirit of the Father and the Spirit of the Son who comes to take up residence in the believer.

7. The Holy Spirit is the guarantee of our inheritance verse 14. Heaven's presence and heavens gifts are already functioning in the believer. Receive your portion today! He will never leave us; He is here to complete the work of Christ in every believer. Until the redemption of the purchased possession

8. All of this is to the praise of His glory.

Jesus taught His disciples that they could not receive all He had to say to them. The things of God do not all come at once. We learn over time as we are able to bear it. Even this teaching will be understood better by some than others because we grow into maturity over time and experience. In John 16, Jesus stated that things would change when the Spirit of Truth would come. He would guide them into all truth. The Spirit of Truth would not speak from His own initiative; He would only speak what He hears from the Father and from the Son. Even in the Godhead, there is an order. The Father sent the Son, the Son made it possible for the promise of the Father to take place, which was the coming of the Holy Spirit to dwell in the believer.

Now, let's consider John 16 and examine what the work of the Holy Spirit is in regard to dealing with the world.

> *Nevertheless I tell you the truth. It is to your advantage that I go away; for if I do not go away, the Helper will not come to you; but if I depart, I will send Him to you. And when He has come, He will convict the world of sin, and of righteousness, and of judgment: of sin, because they do not believe in Me; of righteousness, because I go to My Father and you see Me no more; of judgment, because the ruler of this world is judged.*

John 16:7–11

We have not been left to fight this battle alone. The Holy Spirit is the one who convicts the world, that is, all those in the world. It is the work of the Holy Spirit to convict. Our part is to live and bring the message, but it is by His power that results follow.

The Holy Spirit first convicts of sin. The Bible declares, "For all have sinned, and come short of the glory of God" (Romans 3:23 KJV). "And you were dead in your trespasses and sins" (Ephesians 2:1 NASB 1995). Unfortunately, in today's presentation of the goodness of Christ's forgiveness to unbelievers, this major subject of conviction of sin is neglected. Many are invited to receive Christ for the forgiveness of sin but seldom brought to a conviction of sin. People come to an altar for many reasons, but only one reason matters: we all have sinned and fallen short of the glory of God. We are judged guilty with no hope of our own. The awareness of our sinful condition and how desperately lost we are without Christ is what should be our reason for repentance and asking of God's forgiveness.

Next, the Holy Spirit convicts of righteousness. The goal of salvation is to receive the righteousness of Christ into our life. It is His righteousness that saves and transforms us into His perfect image. We cannot be righteous in our own power or works. Our works, no matter how noble in and of themselves, are simply dead works. The only work that matters is the work of Christ through His death on the cross and through the power of His resurrection life. The conviction of righteousness is seeing our need for His righteousness to be established in our life. It is His grace that produces a life lived in the power He has given to those walking in faith.

> *For by grace you have been saved through faith, and that not of yourselves; it is the gift of God, not of works, lest anyone should boast. For we are His workmanship, created in Christ Jesus for good works, which God prepared beforehand that we should walk in them.*

> Ephesians 2:8-10

Finally, the Holy Spirit convicts of judgment. We need to understand that Christ was judged in our place. The innocent Son of God died for condemned mankind. God, who is the Judge of all, put all of His judgment toward us on His Son to make it possible that we would be reconciled to God and possess His righteousness.

In the judgment that Christ bore for us on the cross and through His descending into hades for us, He carried our sins to hades, removing them as far as the east is from the west. The Psalmist expresses it this way.

> *As far as the east is from the west*
> *So far has He removed our transgressions from us.*

> Psalm 103:12

The present age belongs to Christ and His followers. It is the age of the Spirit (see Joel 2), the age of a new creation on the earth (see

Isaiah 43:19 and 2 Corinthians 5:15). It is the age in which a believer can live by the power of the Holy Spirit because Jesus has overcome the world, the flesh, and the devil.

Next, we will go into more details regarding the work of the Holy Spirit who has sealed us or was given to us as the down payment of our future in Christ, our eternal King.

Revelation 1:16 speaks of the two-edged sword coming from our Lord's mouth. Both His salvation and judgment come through His word. Revelation 1:16 gives the prophetic picture of that word coming from His mouth. We will receive one or the other: salvation or judgment. Many times, man's ideas are added, but the simple truth is either we receive His salvation through the Word and the Spirit of truth, or there is nothing left but His word of judgment.

The Holy Spirit is the essence of the gospel of the kingdom. The disciples were concerned about their nation Israel once again becoming a world kingdom with domination over the nations, so they asked Jesus:

> *"Lord, will You at this time restore the kingdom to Israel?" And He said to them, "It is not for you to know times or seasons which the Father has put in His own authority. But you shall receive power when the Holy Spirit has come upon you; and you shall be witnesses to Me in Jerusalem, and in all Judea and Samaria, and to the end of the earth"*

Acts 1:6-8

The Greek word for "authority" is *exousia* and the Greek word for "power" is *dunamis*. It is where we get the English word *dynamite*. In this context, they are interchangeable. We have been given authority and power against sin and the results of sin, against the kingdom of darkness and to disciple the nations. It is a corporate assignment meant to be done as one new man in Christ through the Holy Spirit. The seal of our inheritance is with authority and power.

Consider how Luke writes about this coming of the Holy Spirit in his Gospel:

> *Then He said to them, "These are the words which I spoke to you while I was still with you, that all things must be fulfilled which were written in the Law of Moses and the Prophets and the Psalms concerning Me." And He opened their understanding, that they might comprehend the Scriptures. Then He said to them, "Thus it is written, and thus it was necessary for the Christ to suffer and to rise from the dead the third day, and that repentance and remission of sins should be preached in His name to all nations, beginning at Jerusalem. And you are witnesses of these things. Behold, I send the Promise of My Father upon you; but tarry in the city of Jerusalem until you are endued with power from on high."*

Luke 24:44-49

Three major apostolic themes in scripture are:

1. The King
2. His kingdom
3. His Spirit

The work of God through the Holy Spirit was given to redeem Israel and establish them on the earth as a new creation of the Holy Spirit. In that first century, only a remnant believed; the rest suffered judgment and destruction.

The Holy Spirit was also given to redeem the Samaritans and the Gentile nations and make them one new man on the earth. He came to establish the Kingdom of God on the earth. The mandate Jesus gave His disciples was to go and disciple the nations. The word *disciple* implies discipline. The discipline of the nations is to bring them under the Reign of Messiah.

What I am speaking about is under the present reign of Christ. It was the work of the Holy Spirit on the earth in the first century, and it continues to be His work today. His plan has not changed. It began with those disciples and it continues through His disciples today.

> *For I am the Lord, I do not change; therefore you are not consumed, O sons of Jacob.*
>
> Malachi 3:6

Ephesians 1:15-23

Therefore I also, after I heard of your faith in the Lord Jesus and your love for all the saints, do not cease to give thanks for you, making mention of you in my prayers: that the God of our Lord Jesus Christ, the Father of glory, may give to you the spirit of wisdom and revelation in the knowledge of Him, the eyes of your understanding being enlightened; that you may know what is the hope of His calling, what are the riches of the glory of His inheritance in the saints, and what is the exceeding greatness of His power toward us who believe, according to the working of His mighty power which He worked in Christ when He raised Him from the dead and seated Him at His right hand in the heavenly places, far above all principality and power and might and dominion, and every name that is named, not only in this age but also in that which is to come.

And He put all things under His feet, and gave Him to be head over all things to the church, which is His body, the fullness of Him who fills all in all.

Ephesians 1:15-23

God Is a Giver, Not a Taker!

Verse 15: The point that Paul made about the believer's inheritance being guaranteed with the sealing of the Holy Spirit provides the basis for what he now teaches. Paul makes the following point, based on the Ephesian believers' faith and love for all the saints.

Verse 16: Paul made it his priority to always give thanks for these believers by "making mention of them in his prayers." This should be our practice as well for the saints that we are in relationship with, such as our shepherd, our leaders in our local church, the other saints we know.

Verses 17 gives his prayer "that the God of our Lord Jesus Christ, the Father of glory, may give to you the spirit of wisdom and revelation in the knowledge of Him."

Lord, please give to us this prayer for others. Cause it to be part of our daily mentioning in our prayer life.

Paul is very precise in what he is saying. "The God of our Lord Jesus Christ." God is the originator of Jesus being the Christ, or Messiah, and being made Lord. "That is Lord of all." Paul expresses this powerful truth when he writes this revelation:

> *Therefore God also has highly exalted Him and given Him the name which is above every name, that at the name of Jesus every knee should bow, of those in heaven, and of those on earth, and of those under the earth, and that every tongue should confess that Jesus Christ is Lord, to the glory of God the Father.*

> Philippians 2:9-11

This is not just Paul's opinion; this is revelation. Paul did not learn this as a Pharisee of Pharisees. Paul received this understanding from the Holy Spirit as the Spirit of Truth opened Paul's mind to the mysteries of the scriptures, that is, the Old Testament's prophetic view toward Messiah's day. The same Holy Spirit wants to help us in our understanding of these important truths as we study and pray over God's word.

The Father of Glory is a New Testament name of God revealed through Paul. The name points to God as the source of glory. Everything about Him is glorious. Glory is an expression of the brilliance of light. It is God who has crowned man with glory. Consider what the writer of Hebrews has to say:

"What is man that You are mindful of him,
Or the son of man that You take care of him?
You have made him a little lower than the angels;
You have crowned him with glory and honor,
And set him over the works of Your hands.
You have put all things in subjection under his feet."
For in that He put all in subjection under him, He left nothing that is not
put under him. But now we do not yet see all things put under him. But
we see Jesus, who was made a little lower than the angels, for the
suffering of death crowned with glory and honor, that He, by the grace
of God, might taste death for everyone

Hebrews 2:6-9

He takes this from Psalm 8:4-6.

John's Gospel helps us to capture the glory of God when he writes:

And the Word became flesh and dwelt among us, and
we beheld His glory, the glory as the only begotten of
the Father, full of grace and truth.

John 1:14

Paul is asking the Father of Glory to give the believers two important gifts, "the spirit of wisdom and revelation in the knowledge of Him" (Christ). Wisdom and revelation come from the Spirit of the Lord. We find recorded in Isaiah 11:2-3 a list of the sevenfold ministry of the Holy Spirit.

1. Rest
2. Wisdom
3. Understanding
4. Counsel
5. Might
6. Knowledge
7. The fear of the Lord

Notice: The Spirit is resting on the promised Son of God, and the promise of the Father is that the Spirit would be given to those who trust in God. That means the sevenfold ministry of the Spirit is also given to believers. Paul, knowing this, prays this prayer for God's people. Do you see what God has for us as His sons and daughters? What He has to give us comes by prayer and faith. Through prayer and faith, an impartation takes place and we receive it as part of the inheritance of God's favor.

Verse 18: Paul is asking that the "eyes of our understanding be enlightened" to know:

1. What is our hope of calling? Always be prepared to give an answer to everyone who asks you to give the reason for the hope that you have. But do this with gentleness and respect (see 1 Peter 3:15).

2. The riches of our inheritance in the saints: abundance of grace; God as our source; every spiritual blessing; rights of a son or daughter; knowing the mystery of His will; redemption through His blood, the forgiveness of sin, to name some.

3. Verse 19: "The exceeding greatness of His power toward us who believe, all according to the working of His mighty power." What power?

4. Verse 20: "Which He worked in Christ when He raised Him from the dead and seated Him at His own right hand in the heavenly places" or realm!

What is the heavenly realm? It is the realm of the throne of God, heavenly Zion, the Jerusalem above.

Verse 21: It is "far above all principality and power and might and dominion." In fact, above "every name that is named, not only in this age" but the age to come.

42

There are three ages we must consider:

1. The Age of Adam: From the beginning to the cross.

2. The Age of the fullness of time: This present age of the New Creation man being raised up, beginning with Christ.

3. The Age to come (ref. 1 Corinthians 2:7-10): God our Father, wants us to have both wisdom and revelation to know presently that:

    And He put all things under His feet, and gave Him to be head over all things to the church, which is His body, the fullness of Him who fills all in all.

    Ephesians 1:22-23

Number 2 above is this present time! O the riches of His grace. O the inheritance of which we have access. Beloved, many are living far beneath the provisions that our great God and King has provided.

The church is His body, not some corporate entity! No, the church is the fullness of Him. Church, let us evaluate how we see things, let that evaluation be by the Word of God through the apostles. How many understand what Paul is proclaiming to the Ephesians? This is not minor, beloved, this is the point of chapter one. "The fullness of Him who fills all in all." This is Messianic. This is God's fullness of purpose in Christ. Let us rethink who we are together as One New Man in Christ Jesus.

Chapter 2 will continue to open Paul's revelation of Christ and of His church and the one new man created by the Holy Spirit.

What Have We Learned?

1. Paul's teachings in these verses are rooted in his understanding of the inheritance we have been guaranteed to receive through the sealing of the Holy Spirit.

2. His prayers for the same spirit of wisdom and revelation that the apostles had concerning the knowledge of Christ.

3. Christ is exalted far above all both in heaven and earth.

4. God's glory is His brilliance of light. There is nothing more glorious than what God has revealed in Christ.

5. We have learned of the Sevenfold Ministries of the Holy Spirit revealed in Isaiah 11:1-2. Those seven ministries rested upon Christ, God's only begotten Son.

6. God wants to open the eyes of our understanding.

7. We considered the Three Ages of scripture: the age of Adam, the age of fullness of time in Christ and the age to come.

8. The church is His body, the fullness of Him.

Chapter 2

Ephesians 2:1-7

*And you He made alive, who were dead in trespasses
and sins, in which you once walked according to the
course of this world, according to the prince of the
power of the air, the spirit who now works in the sons
of disobedience, among whom also we all once
conducted ourselves in the lusts of our flesh, fulfilling
the desires of the flesh and of the mind, and were by
nature children of wrath, just as the others. But God,
who is rich in mercy, because of His great love with
which He loved us, even when we were dead in
trespasses, made us alive together with Christ (by
grace you have been saved), and raised us up together,
and made us sit together in the heavenly places in
Christ Jesus, that in the ages to come He might show
the exceeding riches of His grace in His kindness
toward us in Christ Jesus.*

He Made You Alive

Ephesians 1 through 3:13 is principally about the position of the
Christian in Christ. It is about the Christian as an individual and the
Christian corporately.

The first three verses are humbling and insightful for every
believer with which to come to grips. My experience has taught me that
all Christians knew they were sinners, but most did not think that they
were really that bad of a sinner.

Paul starts in a positive way. "He made you alive, who were dead
in trespasses and sins." I recognize that the statement, "He made you

45

alive" was not in the original Greek. The translators try to help us to grasp the thought being communicated by putting an additional phrase in the text that is implied or communicated later. The point Paul is making is found in verse 5 which deals with life in Christ. It is a wonderful feeling to know you are alive when you could be dead. I am sure many of you have stories you could tell; I know I do. I clearly remember brushing death 3 times. Once, I was almost electrocuted with 2000 volts at about a quarter of an amp. This is enough to put your heart into fibrillation and you die unless it is restarted to pump. It was good to realize I was still alive after the wire broke which was carrying the voltage!

Yes, we were dead in our trespasses and sins, but we are no longer dead in that condition. Life is what the believer has received. That is where our focus needs to be, with humility and gratitude. Many of God's people remain focused on their past sinful condition and not on the life of Christ dwelling within them through the power of the Holy Spirit. The past is the past. We need to lay hold of the *now* and build for the future!

We have used the Sunday pulpit time to preach salvation truths in hope that a visitor will come to Jesus. And many did! Still, we depend too much on the pastor preaching and getting people saved. In fact, the responsibility belongs to each believer in taking the gospel into the world by sharing the good news within their sphere of influence. So, the saints of God need to be equipped fully with what Christ has done for them so their testimony to the world is strong and anointed.

I always try to give those in my audience who do not know Christ an opportunity to come to Christ. At the same time, I recognize the need to equip the saints for the work of ministry—to see produced strong effective believers who are able to share with others the hope they have. Peter instructs us when he said:

> *But sanctify the Lord God in your hearts, and always*
> *be ready to give a defense to everyone who asks you a*

reason for the hope that is in you, with meekness and fear.

1 Peter 3:15

Verse 2: Paul is reminding these Ephesian saints (and us) of their previous lifestyles. Most have not considered what Paul is writing.

1. That our previous life was connected to the course of the world. We think individualistically, but in reality, we are all in the same boat. The old man, or nature, is controlled by the world; family background, culture, education, television, movies and so many other ways.

2. Our life was powered by the "prince of the power of the air." Behind the world is this "prince" Paul speaks about. The true battle was never "flesh and blood, but principalities and powers of darkness." We will study this in greater measure when we get to chapter 6.

3. It is a spirit working in "the sons of disobedience." The influence of the evil behind the world's system gets into people, into their thinking and reasoning, into their emotions and affections, and into their imaginations and memory. It affects their conscience and their sense of right and wrong. All of these areas need to be cleansed by the blood of Jesus and filled with the Holy Spirit and His Word.

Verse 3: Paul makes the point that "we all once conducted ourselves" through four major influences. Note the four levels that Paul mentions.

1. *The lust of the flesh*—rooted in man's fallen nature. That nature was destroyed by Christ (see Romans 6:6-9).

2. *Fulfilling the desires of the flesh*—Christ changed the desires toward heaven's desires (see Colossians 3:1). Can you hear the life side in this scripture? "Raised with Christ."

3. *And of the mind*—Christ came to change our mind. No longer the mindset of the world, away from Christ and heavens will, now we are able to be "conformed to His will" (see Romans 8:28-30).

4. Our nature was *"children of wrath"* (see Ephesians 2:3)—Just like others. The whole human race has the same problem, all have sinned (see Romans 3:23).

The good news in this verse is "but God." Everything turns on these two words. O the riches of God's mercy and great love. Love directed at us! You and me! When did He love us? When we were dead in trespasses! His love did not come after our conversion, but before our encounter with Christ. He knew our problem and it did not hinder His love toward us! He knows our challenges even now and it does not keep Him from loving us. His love is rooted and grounded in Christ, the Rose of Sharon, the perfect Son of God, the accepted sacrifice for sin and the raised-up King who is reigning and ever-living to make intercession for us at God's right hand.

> *Therefore He is also able to save to the uttermost those who come to God through Him, since He always lives to make intercession for them.*

Hebrews 7:25

The writer of Hebrews gives to us great confidence and hope when he wrote:

> *For we do not have a High Priest who cannot sympathize with our weaknesses, but was in all points tempted as we are, yet without sin. Let us therefore come boldly to the throne of grace, that we may obtain mercy and find grace to help in time of need.*

Hebrews 4:15-16

Here is the point: Even when we were dead in trespasses, he made us alive together with Christ.

48

We are saved by grace. We are raised up with all those who have trusted in Christ. Just as Christ was raised from the dead, we have been raised up together to sit with Him in heavenly places in Christ. From God's view, you and I are already raised and seated with Him. Yes, the full manifestation is in the future, but faith dictates we walk presently in the future promises. The future will show "the exceeding riches of His grace for all to see." But those riches of His grace are accessible presently!

The gifts of the Spirit are contained in the exceeding riches of His grace, and the fruit of the Spirit reveals the exceeding riches in our Lord's character. Every promise of God is connected to the exceeding riches. This is surely what Jesus had in mind when He instructed His disciples how to pray. Our prayers are addressed to our Father in heaven, prayer that is rooted in the holiness of His name, prayer that requests for His kingdom to come and for His will to be done on earth as in heaven. Can you see how our future is present in *the here and now* as a result of what God has already done in Christ? Can you understand what Paul understood? We are in Christ and Christ is in God. This is the riches of His grace manifested now and to be fully manifested for all to see in the ages to come (see Colossians 3:1-5).

We are standing in life. Life is our position in Christ. Think life and not death, appreciating all you have been saved from and all that you have been given. Our past life was joined to the course of the world. We were driven by the lusts of our flesh. We were delivered from the prince of the power of the air—the spirit that works in the sons of disobedience.

The enemy wants us to focus on our past. Our mind is renewed to now focus on the life of Christ in us. Everything turns on two words: *"but God."* His riches, mercy, and His great love in that He made a way of escape! His love came when we were dead in our trespasses and sin. His love remains in our present position in Christ. And His love will be displayed for all to see in the ages to come!

Ephesians 2:8-9

For by grace you have been saved through faith, and that not of yourselves; it is the gift of God, not of works, lest anyone should boast.

But God!

These are memory verses for many believers. God's part was His grace. Our part is to respond to His grace by exercising our faith!

Grace is mentioned in over 200 verses. The word *grace* literally means "favor." In Hebrew, it is *chen* from a root word *chanan:* "to bend or stoop in kindness to another as a superior to an inferior" (Strong's 2603). The favor of God has been given to us through His Son, Jesus Christ. God is Sovereign above all, yet He humbled Himself to make it possible for us to be lifted up by redemption and become part of His royal family. Another way of looking at grace is grace-lets. Think of it like jewelry being placed upon us. His nature, His fruit, His gifts—they are all His grace or favor.

Some describe God's grace as unmerited favor. We did nothing in and of ourselves to deserve or earn His favor. It is just because He wanted to give to us His favor or grace. He made grace significant to His plan of redemption. He established His grace for all eternity that there was nothing in us that could or would produce the possibility for God to give us His favor, acceptance and justification. Nothing at all in us!

As I have stated previously, everything turns on the two words which Paul chose to use: "but God!" Remember that His love did not come after our redemption but before, while we were dead in trespasses and sins.

Everything that our heavenly Father does on our behalf is an expression of His grace. God so loved the world, but the world and even His own rejected His love. This makes His grace all the more exceedingly rich toward us. From Noah to you and me! Grace and peace are the greetings through the Apostle John from Jesus to the seven churches of Asia Minor. "Grace to you and peace from Him who is and who was and who is to come" (Revelation 1:4). The final words from John in his letter to the churches (The Book of Revelation) are: "The grace of our Lord Jesus Christ be with you all. Amen." (Revelation 22:21)

The word grace is used over 150 times in the New Testament. The word grace is used some 22 times in the Old Testament and eight of those times, the word grace is found in the book of the Law.

> *Amazing grace*
> *How sweet the sound*
> *That saved a wretch like me*
> *I once was lost, but now I'm found*
> *Was blind, but now I see*
> *'Twas grace that taught my heart to fear*
> *And grace my fears relieved*
> *How precious did that grace appear*
> *The hour I first believed.*

John Newton, 1779

Without His favor or grace, there would be no possibility of exercising faith to trust for our salvation. God acts first, grace, we then receive His grace through faith. Our faith is action back to God for what He has promised and fulfilled in Christ.

> *But without faith it is impossible to please Him, for he*
> *that comes to God must believe that He is, and that He*
> *is a rewarder of those who diligently seek Him.*

Hebrews 11:6

A Few Thoughts About Faith

- Faith is rooted in the faith of Christ.

51

I have been crucified with Christ; it is no longer I who live, but Christ lives in me; and the life which I now live in the flesh I live by the faith in the Son of God, who loved me and gave Himself for me.

Galatians 2:20

- Faith comes in seed form into our regenerated spirit.

Another parable He put forth to them, saying: "The kingdom of heaven is like a mustard seed, which a man took and sowed in his field, which indeed is the least of all the seeds; but when it is grown it is greater than the herbs and becomes a tree, so that the birds of the air come and nest in its branches."

Matthew 13:31-32

(Also referenced in the gospels of Mark and Luke.)

- Faith is developed in our spirit with the goal of changing our minds to trust God in all things. Moving from the conformity of the world to a transformed mind to, "Prove what is that good and acceptable and perfect will of God" (Romans 12:2).

- Faith becomes a lifestyle. "Walk by faith and not by sight" (2 Corinthians 5:7).

- "Faith working through love" (Galatians 5:6).

- Faith can be seen, "When Jesus saw their faith, He said to the paralytic, Son, be of good cheer; your sins are forgiven you" (Matthew 9:2).

- Fearfulness reveals, "Little faith" (see Matthew 8:26).

- Faith is given in particular situations as a gift of the Spirit.

- "Faith comes by hearing and hearing by the Word of God" (Romans 10:17).

- Faith to believe God's word is the very essence of receiving the promises that He says we can have. As a Christian, Romans10:17 gives us knowledge on how faith comes, by taking in God's word. It is when the Word of God becomes a *rhema* word, Or the Word Made Personal–God's *rhema* word is spoken more than once.

For by grace you have been saved through faith, and that not of yourselves; it is the gift of God, not of works, lest anyone should boast.

Ephesians 2:8-9

Ephesians 2:10

For we are His workmanship, created in Christ Jesus for good works, which God prepared beforehand that we should walk in them.

Good Works

We have come into the kingdom of God by grace through faith. It is nothing of ourselves. It is a gift from God. We called it *favor* previously, which is the true meaning of the Hebrew word *chan*. The only place any of us can boast is in the Lord. The Word of God is meant to become *rhema* or "personal." So as the Word of God is formed in us, then faith results.

Now let's turn our attention to verse 10.

Verse 10 follows the point Paul made in verse 9, not our works, for if it was anything about our works, we would boast about our part. It is all about His work. The NKJV uses the word *workmanship*. This is the same word used in most other translations. The word *masterpiece* is used in the New Living Translation.

This is the work of the Holy Spirit, to bring forth a new creation on the earth. Jesus was the first of the new man.

> *And He is the head of the body, the church, who is the beginning, the firstborn from the dead, that in all things He may have the preeminence.*

Colossians 1:18

On the Day of Pentecost, a whole new creation began to develop on the earth. About 3,000 souls were being added to this new creation that came out of the resurrection of Jesus Christ.

Now this work of the Spirit was toward good works. We are speaking of the work that God had prepared before the foundation of the earth. We are not only saved by grace but prepared to work the works of God by grace through faith.

We need to understand that the same grace that God has freely given to us must be given to others through us. His grace is manifested through the fruit of the Holy Spirit. Or what the Holy Spirit is growing up in us to be partaken by others who come in contact with our branch, connected to the vine (see John 15).

Galatians 5 contrasts religious works and the deeds of the world to the Fruit of the Spirit that resides in the believer. The Fruit of the Spirit is what reveals His workmanship; this is the good works along with the gifts or graces of the Spirit. We need to understand the work for which we are called and how to apply that work in our daily life. To do this, we must spend time learning how the Spirit of God is working. Galatians 5:1-26 is invaluable in understanding the process of good works.

> *Stand fast therefore in the liberty by which Christ has made us free, and do not be entangled again with a yoke of bondage. Indeed I, Paul, say to you that if you become circumcised, Christ will profit you nothing. And I testify again to every man who becomes circumcised that he is a debtor to keep the whole law. You have become estranged from Christ, you who attempt to be justified by law; you have fallen from grace. For we through the Spirit eagerly wait for the hope of righteousness by faith. For in Christ Jesus neither circumcision nor uncircumcision avails anything, but faith working through love.*

Galatians 5:1-6

It is religious works that cause one to be separated from Christ! It is faith that endears us to Him and that faith works through love. It is love which fulfills the Law! It is God's type of love that contacts the deeds of the flesh.

You ran well. Who hindered you from obeying the truth? This persuasion does not come from Him who calls you. A little leaven leavens the whole lump. I have confidence in you, in the Lord that you will have no other mind; but he who troubles you shall bear his judgment, whoever he is.

Galatians 5:7-10

Obeying the Truth

Even a little amount of works from our self-efforts causes a leavening in our walk with Christ. Paul tells us here that it has to do with a mindset. Religion troubles us. People who have a religious spirit trouble us. Any kind of religious self-effort is a hindrance to our walking by faith, totally trusting in His work in us.

And I, brethren, if I still preach circumcision, why do I still suffer persecution? Then the offense of the cross has ceased. I could wish that those who trouble you would even cut themselves off!

Galatians 5:11-12

The offense of the cross is in the fact that Christ did everything necessary to reconcile us to God. There is nothing you and I can do to help in our lost situation except to receive God's grace in the work of Christ.

For you, brethren, have been called to liberty; only do not use liberty as an opportunity for the flesh, but through love serve one another. For all the law is fulfilled in one word, even in this: "You shall love your neighbor as yourself." But if you bite and devour one another, beware lest you be consumed by one another!

Galatians 5:13-15

56

It is very important to understand that grace does not give us a license to sin. It frees us from religious efforts to please God, but it empowers us to deal with the flesh and fleshly desires. The workmanship of God in us is a view toward loving our neighbor as we love ourselves. The proof is in the eating of the pudding! Do we enjoy arguing, having to be right, putting another down for their beliefs? Making ourselves look more favorable than others for gain of popularity? Of course, there are many other questions one could ask. Do we bite and devour or do we seek to be a vehicle of love and reconciliation?

Walking In the Spirit

I say then: Walk in the Spirit, and you shall not fulfill the lust of the flesh. For the flesh lusts against the Spirit, and the Spirit against the flesh; and these are contrary to one another, so that you do not do the things that you wish. But if you are led by the Spirit, you are not under the law.

Galatians 5:16-18

Being led by the Spirit does not come from being under the law; a *do this or else* attitude. Rather, it is a manifestation of the life of Christ being lived out through us.

The Contrast

Now the works of the flesh are evident, which are: adultery, fornication, uncleanness, lewdness, idolatry, sorcery, hatred, contentions, jealousies, outbursts of wrath, selfish ambitions, dissensions, heresies, envy, murders, drunkenness, revelries, and the like; of which I tell you beforehand, just as I also told you in time past, that those who practice such things will not inherit the kingdom of God.

Galatians 5:19-21

These are the practices of the flesh that separate us from God and His grace motivated by love that is unfathomable.

> *But the fruit of the Spirit is love, joy, peace, longsuffering, kindness, goodness, faithfulness, gentleness, self-control. Against such there is no law.*

Galatians 5:22-23

Here is found the true character of the godhead, that character as manifested in Christ as He walked in human form on the earth. Paul said in 2 Corinthians 5:16, "That we have known Christ after the flesh," in other words as a human with flesh and bones and blood coursing through His veins. But now we know Him no more that way. Now we know Him as the resurrected Son of God. And that is how we are to know one another, in the power of His resurrected life.

> *But the fruit of the Spirit is love, joy, peace, longsuffering, kindness, goodness, faithfulness, gentleness, self-control. Against such there is no law. And those who are Christ's have crucified the flesh with its passions and desires. If we live in the Spirit, let us also walk in the Spirit. Let us not become conceited, provoking one another, envying one another.*

Galatians 5:22-26

Verses 22-26 are the clearest picture we have of the workmanship of God created in Christ Jesus unto good works. Here we have looked at the nine identifiers of good works in the believers' life. This work is singular, not plural. Fruit, not fruits! His life in us! It is really His character revealed in the believer through this new creation-life we have received from the Holy Spirit.

Verses 24-26 declare that the crucifying of the flesh with its passions and its desires is the way to a daily walk in the Spirit. The instruction from Paul is to not provoke or envy one another. These are the believers' marching orders.

Being His Workmanship

As we continue looking at Ephesians 2:10-13. We are still talking about being His workmanship, created for good works. We saw that the good works are not the works of our own efforts, but His Holy Spirit's work in us. To see this in a deeper way we turned to Galatians 5 and considered the fruit of the Spirit.

It is very important to understand that grace does not give us license to sin. It frees us from religious efforts to please God and empowers us to deal with the flesh and fleshly desires. The workmanship of God in us is a view toward loving our neighbor as we love ourselves. The proof is in the eating of the pudding! Do we enjoy arguing, having to be right, putting another down for their beliefs? Making ourselves look more favorable than another for gain of popularity? And of course, many other questions one could ask. Do we bite and devour or do we seek to be a vehicle of love and reconciliation? Good works because it is God's work in the believer.

Five areas that can help us enter into His workmanship:

1. Be familiar with the principles of scripture.

2. Daily asking the Lord for His guidance.

3. Learning to recognize His voice.

4. Opening your heart to do His will.

5. Be obedient to His clear teachings found in scripture.

Walking In the Spirit

Walking in the Spirit is the answer to a victory over the flesh.

> *I say then: Walk in the Spirit, and you shall not fulfill the lust of the flesh.*

> *But if you are led by the Spirit, you are not under the
> law.*

Galatians 5:16, 18

As we said earlier, being led by the Spirit does not come from being under the law. It is a manifestation of the life of Christ being lived out through us. It is His life in us focused on others. It is a giveaway ministry. We give away to others what He has given to us, yet we retain all that we have received from Him by grace through faith. Can you see how this is so far beyond our human nature? It comes from the supernatural nature of Christ's life in us, motivated by love, putting others above ourselves.

Joy is generated out of His love. Not separate from love, but the supernatural results of loving as He loved us. This means giving our best so others might gain. The Bible calls this "joy inexpressible."

> *In this you greatly rejoice, though now for a little
> while, if need be, you have been grieved by various
> trials, that the genuineness of your faith, being much
> more precious than gold that perishes, though it is
> tested by fire, may be found to praise, honor, and glory
> at the revelation of Jesus Christ, whom having not
> seen you love. Though now you do not see Him, yet
> believing, you rejoice with joy inexpressible and full of
> glory, receiving the end of your faith—the salvation of
> your souls.*

1 Peter 1:6-9

From that joy, peace is manifested, peace that is beyond human effort and works. There is no peace outside of this kind of love and joy. Now, we hear a lot about praying for the peace of Jerusalem, taken from Psalm 122:6. The peace of Jerusalem is not a natural kind of peace worked out by governments. In fact, it's not speaking about what most think. It is a prayer that was answered when the Prince of Peace came and walked the streets of Jerusalem two thousand years ago. A remnant believed and received God's peace-person, Christ Jesus, but the majority of that generation rejected God's peace offering. What followed was anything but peace in the destruction of Jerusalem and its temple worship and the scattering of the tribes of Israel among the nations.

Now peace comes from the heavenly Jerusalem where Christ sits and reigns from above. And that peace resides in each believer by grace through faith. Believers who are now "living stone" built together as a "holy temple" in the Lord, the believers make up the holy nation redeemed by the blood of the Lamb! Peter in 1 Peter 2:5-9 lays this out in his epistle. We must come back to what those apostles understood.

Consider what follows peace in Galatians 5:22-23.

> *But the fruit of the Spirit is love, joy, peace, longsuffering, kindness, goodness, faithfulness, gentleness, self-control. Against such there is no law.*

And those who are Christ's have crucified the flesh with its passions and desires. This is the good work of God. The flesh needs to die daily so that the resurrection life of Christ might be manifested. The key is daily crucifying the flesh. "If we live in the Spirit, let us also walk in the Spirit" (Galatians 5:25). The life we possess from heaven is the Life of Christ, which comes from the Holy Spirit at work in us, "To both will and to do according to His good pleasure" (Philippians 2:13).

"Let us not become conceited, provoking one another, envying one another" (Galatians 5:26). The work of God is a work that must be done in humility. One of our biggest challenges is the pride of life. The only thing that can bring forth the will of God is to crucify the flesh with its lusts. Only that will make room for the Life of Christ to be fully released.

Remember, it is by grace through faith, not of our works, but his work completed in Christ Jesus!

Ephesians 2:11-13

Therefore remember that you, once Gentiles in the flesh—who are called Uncircumcision by what is called the Circumcision made in the flesh by hands—that at that time you were without Christ, being aliens from the commonwealth of Israel and strangers from the covenants of promise, having no hope and without God in the world. But now in Christ Jesus you who once were far off have been brought near by the blood of Christ.

Strangers From the Covenants of Promise

The word, therefore, causes us to reflect on what had been said previously. Paul spoke of grace, faith, and workmanship created in Christ Jesus for good works.

Beginning in verse 11, Paul calls these Ephesian believers to remember that they were Gentiles in the flesh. We all had our beginning in the flesh. In this case, Paul is making a distinction between Gentiles (or uncircumcision) and those who were called the circumcision made in the flesh by hands—also known as Jews.

There was a time when these Gentile believers were without Christ. Before Christ, they were aliens, not connected to the commonwealth of Israel. Not only that, they were strangers from the covenants of promise, having no hope and without God.

These are important points that Paul is addressing. Many do not understand what Paul understood and what he is saying to these Ephesian Christians, and by the way, to us! The distinction between Israel and all the other nations was the Covenants of Promise. The hope was contained in the certainty of the promises which God had given to Abraham and given to his descendants. Those promises are found in the Law, the Prophets, the Psalms and the Books of Wisdom.

Paul's writing is critical to properly understand the work God the Father has accomplished in Christ Jesus. Christ Jesus is the centrality of the Good News of the Kingdom. It is not organized church. It is not some so-called restoration of natural Israel. Both of those subjects have divided the church throughout the centuries. The organized church rejected the foundation Paul and the other apostles built in their lifetimes. Those apostles built the true foundation, which was described by the prophets of the Old Testament. This is mentioned in Ephesians 2:19-20:

> *Now, therefore, you are no longer strangers and foreigners, but fellow citizens with the saints and members of the household of God, having been built upon the foundation of apostles and prophets, Jesus Christ Himself being the chief cornerstone.*

By the third century, the bishop became the focus. This belief grew until we had the Bishop of Rome or the Pope, the so-called, Christ's equal here on earth. The church had become imperialistic and Roman.

> Imperial: the policy of extending the rule or authority of an empire or nation over foreign countries, or of acquiring and holding colonies and dependencies. advocacy of imperial or sovereign interests over the interests of the dependent states. imperial government; rule by an emperor or empress.
>
> Dictionary.com

Eventually, in the 1500s we had the beginning of the Reformation. The church did need reforming, but the reformation did not take us all the way back to what the Apostles of Christ gave to us. The Reformation broke up the Imperial Church of Rome, but it gave us a church that was run by the State. In many cases throughout Europe, a King became the head of these Protestant churches. That system drove many to flee the oppression created under this apostate religious system. A new thing was begun in what became America. The new thing became known as religious freedom. Down through the centuries we have experienced the church slowly being turned back to what our Lord had in mind. He is not done yet reviving His church.

When we get to Ephesians 4, we will learn what Paul understood about the church and the goal of a mature people manifesting the full stature of Christ.

The separation of church and state in America was rooted in the denominational system that the church had morphed into. The separation clause had nothing to do with keeping Christianity out of the public square, but everything to do with no Christian denomination becoming The Church of America. The Founders used the word *religion* to speak of the individual denominations, not the plural use of the word as it is used today to refer to all religions.

My conviction and prophetic sense are that much of which is taking place today is the Lord Himself rearranging the systems of this world, including the church, with a view of reforming and bringing us back to what His apostles understood so that He will have a church built on the foundation that those apostles laid. He is reshaping His church so she can effectively disciple the nations. He is also reshaping the nations so they might be readied to receive the true message of the good news of Christ's kingdom. There will be a future harvesting of the nations which truly belong to the Son of God and His Kingdom purposes.

> *Praise the Lord, all you Gentiles!*
> *Laud Him, all you peoples!*
> *For His merciful kindness is great toward us,*
> *And the truth of the Lord endures forever.*
> *Praise the Lord!*

> Psalms 117:1-2

The apostles of Christ understood that Jesus had come to first redeem Israel, to reconstitute Israel to be the one holy nation with Jesus the Christ as King seated on David's throne in heaven. Just as God had promised David, He would do by placing his seed on an eternal throne (see 2 Samuel 7:8-17). God had purposed that Israel would be the nation that would bring the other nations into God's plan. This is at the heart of Peter's message in Acts 2 and in Peter's first epistle, 1 Peter 2:1-9.

Here in Ephesians 2:11-13, Paul is telling Gentile Christians that they have been made part of God's eternal plan. They were aliens from the commonwealth of Israel. They were strangers from the covenants of promise. They had no hope. They were without God and in the world, but now in Christ Jesus, they who once were far off have been brought near by the blood of Christ.

Can you see what Paul is saying? The true Israel is those who have received Christ as Messiah, beginning with those Jews who received the new circumcision, not with the hands of the flesh but through the blood of Jesus Christ. Now believing Gentiles have been circumcised (set apart) by the same blood, producing the circumcision of the heart. We are now included in the commonwealth of Israel and we are also now the partakers of the covenants of promise.

> *In Him you were also circumcised with the circumcision made without hands, by putting off the body of the sins of the flesh, by the circumcision of Christ, buried with Him in baptism, in which you also were raised with Him through faith in the working of God, who raised Him from the dead.*
>
> Colossians 2:11-12
>
> *For we are the circumcision, who worship God in the Spirit, rejoice in Christ Jesus, and have no confidence in the flesh, though I also might have confidence in the flesh.*
>
> Philippians 3:3-4

As we continue, we will see how Paul develops this thinking and concludes with the understanding of making both one. That is Jew and Gentile, through one Spirit, built upon the foundation of the apostles and prophets.

I hope you are grasping what Paul has been emphasizing up to this point. Everything is summed up in Christ Jesus. He is all in all. God's plan has always been a people coming out of Christ's redemptive work producing good works. That is the good works of God's plan created by His Holy Spirit. Each person who receives this grace of God (His favor) and responds through faith becomes part of God's glorious work on the earth. Father God is connecting heaven and earth in one holy apostolic nation which exalts Christ as King of Kings and Lord of Lords and fills the earth with Christ's kingdom.

Ephesians 2:13-18

But now in Christ Jesus you who once were far off have been brought near by the blood of Christ. For He Himself is our peace, who has made both one, and has broken down the middle wall of separation, having abolished in His flesh the enmity, that is, the law of commandments contained in ordinances, so as to create in Himself one new man from the two, thus making peace, and that He might reconcile them both to God in one body through the cross, thereby putting to death the enmity. And He came and preached peace to you who were afar off and to those who were near. For through Him we both have access by one Spirit to the Father.

True Blood

Note that *enmity* speaks of being actively opposed or hostile to someone or something.

Let's begin by considering God's creation man. The entire human race has the blood of Adam coursing through their veins. This blood becomes red when it comes in contact with air which contains life-giving oxygen. Every human being has the same experience regardless of their individual race.

So also, the blood of the last Adam, Jesus Christ, cleanses from all unrighteousness when by faith a son of Adam receives the power of Christ's life-giving blood. His blood is available to connect individuals throughout the entire human race as one holy body, His body, created by the Holy Spirit. His blood fulfills all the covenants of promise given to Abraham and his sons, Isaac and Jacob, and reaffirmed to the heads of the tribes of Israel. Not all of the descendants of Abraham are in line to receive the covenants of promise as made clear by Jesus when He confronted the apostate leaders of Israel in John 8:33-47. Consider John

8:37, "I know that you are Abraham's descendants, but you seek to kill Me, because My word has no place in you." Then in John 8:39, Jesus says, "If you were Abraham's children, you would do the works of Abraham." Then in John 8:42, Jesus said to them, "If God were your Father, you would love me, for I proceed forth and came from God; nor have I come of Myself, but He sent Me."

Can you see how important Christ's blood is in fulfilling the covenants and the promises? Not even the natural descendants of Abraham, even religious leaders, could enter into the promises without the true blood of the covenant. Being a Jew does not matter now, nor anything else. Only the blood of Jesus can save, cleanse, and heal from the brokenness caused by sin.

Let's consider what Paul is teaching the churches of Galatia.

Now to Abraham and his Seed were the promises made. He does not say, "And to seeds," as of many, but as of one, "And to your Seed," who is Christ.

Galatians 3:16

Your seed is the promise, not millions of children or millions of Jews, but one. That one is Christ! This is how Jesus could separate descendants from children in John 8. Many today are confused with the reestablishment of the State of Israel. Even today, only those Jews or citizens of the state of Israel who trust in the blood of Christ for their redemption are the children of promise. They are the true circumcision, not of the flesh, but of the Spirit.

Galatians 3:26-29 sums up what I am saying:

For you are all sons of God through faith in Christ Jesus. For as many of you as were baptized into Christ have put on Christ. There is neither Jew nor Greek, there is neither slave nor free, there is neither male nor female; for you are all one in Christ Jesus. And if you are Christ's, then you are Abraham's seed, and heirs according to the promise.

Peace

Now that we have established through verse 13 of Ephesians 2 and with the help of the Galatian passages, that the blood of the covenant is in Christ Jesus' shed blood, let's look at our personal standing and what we have been given as sons and daughters of covenant.

Verse 14: "For He Himself is our peace!" Peace is personal, peace is a covenant right of every believer. This peace flows out of His love for us. The peace of Jerusalem is found in a man, the man Christ Jesus, the Prince of Peace. Man in his own efforts can never produce true peace. But the blood of Christ shed for mankind has that power to establish peace beyond all knowledge and understanding.

The peace of Christ made both one and has broken down the middle wall of separation. What is the wall of separation? It is the law of commandments contained in ordinances. One of the ordinances was that of circumcision of the flesh. God no longer sees a separation between Jew and Gentile. Both need the blood of Jesus to be saved and made sons of Abraham. Both Jew and Gentile alike need the blood of Christ through the abolishing in His flesh the enmity which is the law of commandments contained in ordinances.

The peace that Christ produced in Himself is the peace of one new man. From the two, Christ made one new man. A whole new creation was birthed in His resurrection. The true Israel of God is now in Christ who fulfilled the covenants of promise through His shed blood and resurrection life given to all those who believe!

Herein lays the answer to the divisions in the body of Christ. Herein lays the answer to the racial divide. He is our peace who has broken down the middle wall of separation. He did this to reconcile them both to God. Jew and Gentile reconciled to God. He is the reconciliation for the entire human race. That reconciliation is in one body through the cross, thereby putting to death the enmity.

Our message of peace comes because of the work of Jesus' cross. Believers are mandated to preach to all, both Jew and Gentile, that is, all the races throughout the earth. "For through Him, we both have access by one Spirit to the Father" (Ephesians 2:18).

There are two things that unite us. First is our receiving together the bread and the cup—His broken body and His shed blood. The second is receiving His Holy Spirit in the fullness of the work He brings. One new man created in Christ Jesus the Lord. Salvation is personal, but it is also corporate.

> *Endeavoring to keep the unity of the Spirit in the bond of peace. There is one body and one Spirit, just as you were called in one hope of your calling; one Lord, one faith, one baptism; one God and Father of us all, who is above all, and through all, and in you all.*

> Ephesians 4:3-6

Ephesians 2:18: "For through Him we both have access by one Spirit to the Father." Paul can be deep in what he says, but also he has the gift of being simplistic. This verse sums up what we have been learning: both Jew and Gentile have access through the one Holy Spirit. The Holy Spirit came to convict the world of sin, righteousness, and judgment. There is no special group on this side of the cross. The blood of Jesus evened the field. Jew and Gentile are treated exactly the same now. The Jews were used to giving us the promises of covenant. They were the vehicle, but the promise of the Seed was to all who would trust as Abraham trusted. "Abraham rejoiced to see My day, and he saw it and was glad" (John 8:56).

We too rejoice with faithful Abraham, the father of all who trust in Christ! He is the one who is heir of the promise and covenants. As God promised Abraham, "In you all the nations shall be blessed" (Galatians 3:8).

Ephesians 2:19-22

Now, therefore, you are no longer strangers and foreigners, but fellow citizens with the saints and members of the household of God, having been built on the foundation of the apostles and prophets, Jesus Christ Himself being the chief cornerstone, in whom the whole building, being fitted together, grows into a holy temple in the Lord, in whom you also are being built together for a dwelling place of God in the Spirit.

The Mystery Revealed

Notice the word: *therefore*. What must we do when we encounter that word? You guessed it—go back and make sure you understand what proceeded it.

Now in Christ, as promised to Abraham, there is no difference between Jew and Gentile. The promise to Abraham is directly connected to Christ as the seed, the ultimate promise. Everything is now seen in Christ. All the nations are included because of the reconciling blood of Christ.

Whichever Gentile race you have come from, you are no longer a stranger. The blessings are toward all who trust in Christ, who receive Him as God's eternal king. Those from every nation who come to Christ and receive God's perfect gift to mankind become "fellow citizens with the saints." Saints are any that have been redeemed by Christ's blood. Saints are not some special class, but each believer that has been sanctified or separated to God by the Holy Spirit falls into the definition of saints. Every saint is a member of God's household. That household began with Abraham. It increased through Isaac and Jacob. Jacob was renamed Israel, meaning Prince with God. He was renamed by the angel with whom he wrestled as recorded in Genesis 32:28.

71

Jacob had 12 sons who became the heads of the 12 tribes of Israel. The tribes enlarged in Egypt for 400 years until Moses led them out toward the land of Canaan, the land promised to their father Abraham. They became the nation of Israel. They were known as the House of Moses who had given to them God's written law, which he received from God as written with God's own fingers.

The New Testament is about a change in headship. Christ Jesus becomes the firstborn of those raised from the dead and is seated on His Father's throne in heaven. Jesus is known as David's Son and heir to David's throne. He now reigns as King of kings and is rising up His household made up of the redeemed, taken out of every kindred and tribe among the nations. Thus, all the saints are part of His household, the household of God. The redeemed Israel was redeemed by the Seed of Abraham. The redeemed Israel is ruled over by the Seed of David. They are one and the same, the Seed of Abraham and the Seed of David which was the promise of God in covenant with these two men. (See Hebrews 10 for more insight to what Christ Jesus has accomplished.)

Beloved, you are part of the greatest plan and purpose made in heaven and being worked out on earth. Ephesians 2:20 reveals the foundation of this plan. The foundation is in the apostles that God gave to Jesus and in all the prophets of the Old Covenant who point to Messiah's day.

This is not a scripture to be skimmed over quickly! If we do not understand this verse, we will build religious systems and not the church that Christ is building. The foundations that the apostles of Christ gave to us are the only foundations that can support the Lord's work. The apostles, through the gift of the Holy Spirit, were able to understand the writings of the prophets of old. They rightly interpreted the Old Testament scripture concerning Christ and what He had come to do.

The entire New Testament is the revelation of the Old Testament. It is a type and shadow of the Old Testament writers. God hid the mysteries of the kingdom in their writings. The apostles were given the keys to unlock those mysteries and make clear the plan that God had possessed from the beginning concerning Christ and a redeemed people who would carry out His will. These are the "keys of the kingdom" which Christ promised His disciples in Matthew 16:19.

With Christ as the cornerstone, the building is built and fitted together, growing into a holy temple. Remember that this building is not mortar and brick. It is a living, breathing, holy structure fitted together with "living stones" (1 Peter 2:1-9).

Now Paul really makes it personal when he says "in whom you also are being built together." This is why unity is so vital. This gives light to Psalm 133. Unity is about what God is building through Christ. It is one new man on the earth; one royal priesthood, and one holy nation.

God has been looking for a dwelling place to dwell in the Holy Spirit. The greatest picture is the New Jerusalem descending from heaven as revealed in the Book of Revelation. "A glorious church not having spot or wrinkle or any such thing," as Paul puts it in Ephesians 5:27. Everything we do corporately needs to have this in mind: God's goal, God's purpose, which is everything complete in Christ.

Are you fitted together? Do you know where you are joined in Christ? I am not speaking of some church membership; I am speaking of relationships that you know the Spirit of the Lord has established. I have long-term relationships with people, some of whom I do not see often, but the life of Christ flows through those relationships. I am strengthened, I have grown in Christ, and I am more effective in my Christian life as a result of those relationships that the Holy Spirit has formed over a lifetime.

I hope, for those reading this book, you find this writing helpful in clarifying significant relationships in life. Many of you I will never meet, but through this means of communication, we are joined together in God's greater plan. You are fitted with others as well and carry what you are learning in order to share with others through words and through your lifestyle. We are fitted together by the Spirit to grow up as mature men and women in Christ. The Spirit of God is dwelling in you and He is dwelling in me. We are His dwelling place to witness of His love to the world.

Next, we begin Ephesians 3. We will begin to learn more about the mystery that the apostle Paul understood through the gift of grace that was given to him. This is core teaching for a fuller understanding of God's plan and purpose being worked in your own life and ministry to others.

Chapter 3

Ephesians 3:1-7

For this reason I, Paul, the prisoner of Christ Jesus for you Gentiles—if indeed you have heard of the dispensation of the grace of God which was given to me for you, how that by revelation He made known to me the mystery (as I have briefly written already, by which, when you read, you may understand my knowledge in the mystery of Christ), which in other ages was not made known to the sons of men, as it has now been revealed by the Spirit to His holy apostles and prophets: that the Gentiles should be fellow heirs, of the same body, and partakers of His promise in Christ through the gospel, of which I became a minister according to the gift of the grace of God given to me by the effective working of His power.

More Mystery Revealed

The phrase: *For this reason*, is like the word *therefore*. One needs to be rooted and grounded in the previous understanding that Paul had written about. Rooted and grounded is a good measurement of becoming solid in the scriptures. It is not wise to just skim over verses and then maybe land on a favorite verse. This is not studying the scriptures as Paul describes to his disciple Timothy.

Be diligent to present yourself approved to God, a worker who does not need to be ashamed, rightly dividing the word of truth.

2 Timothy 2:15

Much of the confusion regarding the teachings of scripture is from poor ways of studying God's Word. The technical word for this is *hermeneutics*. Many collect scriptures to prove a point of doctrine, but they fail to consider other scriptures that bring a more complete understanding of what the Word of God is communicating. My stand on this subject is to interpret scripture in the light of what the apostles of Christ understood. Having said this, let's go back to what the apostle Paul is communicating in these verses.

Paul first speaks of his present situation, which was being in a Roman prison. His attitude was that he was really the "prisoner of Christ Jesus for you Gentiles." This communicates Paul's total surrender to Christ and His lordship. Paul was a man that Jesus could completely rely upon to represent the cause of Christ Jesus perfectly well!

In verse 2, Paul turns his attention to what these Ephesian Christians should know and understand. That understanding related to what God had given to Paul, not man but God. *"If indeed you have heard of the dispensation of the grace of God which was given to me for you."* Paul is saying he received grace or favor or a gift from God for the Gentiles.

What were the means by which Paul received this grace? It was by revelation. A revelation is something that did not come by natural means, but rather by the Spirit of God. Paul was given the ability to understand the mystery. A mystery is something hidden that begs to be discovered. All that Paul had already said was a brief description of this mystery. Please understand that Ephesians 1 and 2 are not the ramblings of somebody in prison trying to pass the time away but the depths of Christ beginning to be unfolded.

Verse 4: "By which, when you read, you may understand my knowledge in the mystery of Christ." Paul was uniquely chosen by Christ for the task of "understanding the mystery of Christ." Why not Peter or John or James? The Bible does not specifically tell us, but permit me a guess. Paul, with his absolute dedication to the law, his zealousness to the point of persecuting the saints, even consenting to the stoning of Stephen, demonstrated a commitment beyond others to serve to the uttermost what he understood as honoring God.

Verse 5: "Which in other ages was not made known to the sons of men, as it has now been revealed by the Spirit to His holy apostles and prophets."

Ecclesiastes 3:1 states: "There is a time for everything, and a season for every activity under heaven." This verse speaks of natural things, but the principle applies to spiritual matters as well. God reveals His mysteries in His own timing. The mysteries of which Paul is speaking are found throughout the Old Testament, but until the Spirit of God was ready to give revelation to His apostles, those mysteries remained hidden, even to God's chosen people. They remained hidden even to Saul when he was a Pharisee of Pharisees persecuting the Lord's church before his Damascus Road experience with Jesus. Those mysteries are part of the keys of the kingdom of which Jesus spoke about in Matthew 16:19 as I mentioned previously. Without this revelation of the mystery, one cannot fully understand the New Testament.

The understanding of the mysteries of which Paul is speaking and the keys of the kingdom that Jesus promised to give to His apostles are vital to both the apostolic and prophetic New Testament ministry gifts. Every Fivefold minister should be familiar with these essential foundational understandings. The apostolic and prophetic ministries are intended to unlock the mysteries through the understanding of the keys of the kingdom by the grace the Holy Spirit gives.

Verse 6: "That the Gentiles should be fellow heirs, of the same body, and partakers of His promises in Christ through the gospel." Can you begin to see how important chapter 2 is regarding the one new man, and also the Gentiles being joined to the redeemed Israel as fellow citizens with the redeemed Jews? The gospel is very incomplete without this revelation of God's grace!

The Lord is not just saving individuals for heaven. He is creating His body by the Holy Spirit. Without this corporate understanding, the message of the gospel of the Kingdom of God is incomplete and opens the door for many erroneous interpretations and doctrines that are not of God. In our study, we are examining the foundation of the Lord's work. The taller the building, the deeper the foundation must be dug, all the way to bedrock. Even if the earth shakes and moves, the structure will not give way. Can you understand in the light of what Paul is teaching, why there are so many doctrines that divide the body of Christ?

Finally, our teaching takes us to verse 7 where Paul helps us to understand his ministry in gifting terms. His ministry came from God as a gift of grace. This grace gift came as an effective work of His power. Without God's power, nothing really happens. Paul is not writing out of his natural understanding of God's purposes but by the gift of God that he was given. He calls that gift the grace of God. Only what is done by God's power will bring forth eternal substance and lasting results.

What Have We Learned?

1. The importance of being rooted and grounded. Not just skimming over scripture, but understanding the "building blocks that God uses to establish the Word of God in us.

2. Scripture must be interpreted in the light of what the apostles understood. Paul appeals to what these Ephesians should know.

3. Paul received revelation by the grace of God, which was a gift given by God.

4. That grace was the ability to reveal the mysteries of God which were hidden in the Old Testament writings by the prophets (v4).

5. It was by grace through faith that the mysteries could be received and believed through the preaching of the apostles.

6. That mystery was, "That the Gentiles should be fellow heirs, of the same body, and partakers of His promises in Christ through the gospel" (v6).

7. The Lord is not just saving individuals; He is creating a body for Christ from every nation and tribe under heaven.

Ephesians 3:8-13

To me, who am less than the least of all the saints, this grace was given, that I should preach among the Gentiles the unsearchable riches of Christ, and to make all see what is the fellowship of the mystery, which from the beginning of the ages has been hidden in God who created all things through Jesus Christ; to the intent that now the manifold wisdom of God might be made known by the church to the principalities and powers in the heavenly places, according to the eternal purpose which He accomplished in Christ Jesus our Lord, in whom we have boldness and access with confidence through faith in Him. Therefore I ask that you do not lose heart at my tribulations for you, which is your glory.

Purpose of the Mystery

We have learned about the mystery revealed. Now we will learn about the purpose of the mystery. The mystery is that God always intended to bring the Gentiles into His purpose which He created in Christ Jesus our Lord. Remember what verse 6 stated,

> *That the Gentiles should be fellow heirs, of the same body, and partakers of His promises in Christ through the gospel.*

A very important fact to remember is that we have fellowship with the apostles through their teachings. Their teachings point us to the true fellowship that is with the Father and His Son Jesus Christ (see 1 John 1:3).

God always had in mind a new creation of the Spirit. This is at the heart of the resurrection. This is what Jesus was speaking about with Nicodemus as recorded in John 3:3, "Most assuredly, I say to you, unless one is born again, he cannot see the kingdom of God." Nicodemus wants to know how this can be. So, Jesus explains in John 3:6, "That which is born of the flesh is flesh, and that which is born of the Spirit is spirit."

The flesh speaks of God's first creation man, which was Adam. In the Garden, God created Adam and breathed into Adam's nostrils the breath of life and man became a living soul. In the resurrection of Christ, a new life was given to man, the life of the Spirit which gave man eternal life through the Spirit. In the receiving of the Holy Spirit, God's gift and His down payment of the inheritance, we receive eternal life.

Paul writes in 1 Corinthians 15 about this new man in Christ.

> *But now Christ is risen from the dead, and has become the first fruits of those who have fallen asleep.*
>
> 1 Corinthians 15:20

The blessed hope of the church is the glorious return of Jesus Christ who will bring with Him all those who have fallen asleep in Christ. He will also draw to Himself all those who are alive on earth when He returns. It is important for us to look closer at 1 Corinthians 15 and study the whole chapter if we want to more clearly understand what God has accomplished in Christ and the purpose of the mystery that is in Christ.

> *For since by man came death, by Man also came the resurrection of the dead. For in Adam all die, even so in Christ all shall be made alive.*
>
> 1 Corinthians 15:21-22

Dropping down to verse 45 we read,

> *And so it is written, "The first man Adam became a living being.' The last Adam became a life-giving spirit."*

In verse 8 of Ephesians 3, Paul identifies what has been given to him for the Gentiles. His message by preaching to the Gentiles was nothing less than "The unsearchable riches of Christ." What is Paul describing? He is describing what nobody understood until Christ fulfilled all that the prophets had foretold regarding His coming and the establishing of His kingdom on earth through the Holy Spirit's resurrection power—that power to create a new man created in the image of Christ Jesus.

Jesus brought an end to sin and death that had cursed the whole human race. Satan had the keys, but Jesus took them back. He had made it possible for a new creation to begin to inhabit the earth, a new creation from every nation (see 2 Corinthians 5:17). The eternal life in us is the life of God. Our identity is no longer in Adam but in the last Adam who is Christ the Lord. Paul in Romans said it like this,

> *But if the Spirit of Him who raised Jesus from the dead dwells in you, He who raised Christ from the dead will also give life to your mortal bodies through His Spirit who dwells in you.*

> Romans 8:11

The Fellowship of the Mystery

Did you know that our fellowship is a mystery? Do you remember what Acts 2:41-42 says concerning the new believers?

> *Then those who gladly received his word were baptized; and that day about three thousand souls were added to them. And they continued steadfastly in the apostles' doctrine and fellowship, in the breaking of bread, and in prayers.*

This fellowship is a whole new administration that Christ has come to establish for His house. The fellowship is no longer a fellowship around the law and rituals. It is now fellowship around grace that comes from Messiah's overcoming the world, the flesh, and the devil. It comes from His kingly reign in heaven at the right hand of the Father through the gift of the Holy Spirit.

What Peter preached in Acts 2, which these 3,000 believers received as the truth of God, was the clear message that Jesus, whom they had crucified, God had raised up and made Him both Lord and Christ. Their fellowship was rooted in what the Old Testament prophets proclaimed of Christ's coming and that fulfillment. It was in the power of the Holy Spirit in them. Many in that day rejected the good news of the gospel, the good news that Messiah is presently reigning as King of kings and Lord of lords. The good news was that heaven had come to earth in the person of the Holy Spirit.

By Acts 10, the gospel had included the Gentiles, and the mystery of the kingdom had been fully realized. Paul sees this as a redeemed Israel which now includes the Gentile nations which receive Christ as God's promised redeemer and King. Consider how Paul ends his letter to the Galatians:

> *And as many as walk according to this rule, peace and*
> *mercy be upon them, and upon the Israel of God.*

> Galatians 6:16

Only the Holy Spirit can reveal what God has in His mind. Consider what Paul said to both the Romans and the Corinthian believers about the mind of God:

> *Oh, the depth of the riches both of the wisdom and*
> *knowledge of God! How unsearchable are His*
> *judgments and His ways past finding out!*

> *For who has known the mind of the Lord?*
> *Or who has become His counselor?*
> *Or who has first given to Him*
> *And it shall be repaid to him?"*

For of Him and through Him and to Him are all things, to whom be glory forever. Amen.

Romans 11:33-36

These things we also speak, not in words which man's wisdom teaches but which the Holy Spirit teaches, comparing spiritual things with spiritual. But the natural man does not receive the things of the Spirit of God, for they are foolishness to him; nor can he know them, because they are spiritually discerned. But he who is spiritual judges all things, yet he himself is rightly judged by no one. For "who has known the mind of the Lord that he may instruct Him?" But we have the mind of Christ.

1 Corinthians 2:13-16

It was always in the mind of God to redeem the world. His purpose has been to create one new man in Christ Jesus. It was His plan to move mankind from the natural realm to the supernatural realm. He accomplished all this through the cross and in the resurrection. He began anew when He poured out the Holy Spirit on the day of Pentecost. He began the new thing that Isiah 43:19-21 spoke about concerning Christ in the redemption of Israel on the Day of Pentecost when 3,000 brethren believed and drank of the living water. He continued the work with believing Samaritans as recorded in Acts 8. He completed His plan when the Gentiles believed and received His Holy Spirit just like the Jews and Samaritans had. His work continues today with the same religious battles on the earth. He is reviving His church, His holy nation redeemed by the blood of the Lamb.

What Have We Learned?

1. We are establishing an understanding of the purpose of the mystery.

2. God always had in His mind a new creation of the Spirit.

3. The flesh speaks of the first creation in Adam and his fall.

4. The resurrection gives way to a new creation of the Spirit that begins with Israel and the covenants of promise. Then moves to the Samaritans, and finally the Gentile nations.

5. Paul was given the assignment to preach to the Gentiles, "the unsearchable riches of Christ."

6. This is what all the prophets foretold regarding the coming of Messiah and the establishment of His Kingdom on the earth.

7. Jesus brought an end to sin and death. The eternal life in every believer is the life of God (Zoe) life in the absolute

8. Our fellowship is in the apostle's doctrine and the fellowship they enjoyed (see 1 John 1:3).

Here Is the Purpose and The Fellowship of The Mystery

God always had in His mind a new creation of the Spirit. The flesh speaks of the first creation in Adam and his fall. The resurrection gives way to a new creation of the Spirit that begins with Israel and the covenants of promise. The issue for Paul and the other apostles specifically, had to do with the law and the new administration that Christ established, making it possible for the Gentiles to be counted as part of the Israel of God through His shed blood and the infilling of His Holy Spirit. Through Christ's sacrifice and the outpouring of the Holy Spirit, it became possible for the Samaritans and finally the Gentile nations to be joined to the commonwealth of Israel.

Paul was given the assignment to preach to the Gentiles the unsearchable riches of Christ. This is what all the prophets foretold regarding the coming of Messiah and the establishment of His Kingdom on the earth. Jesus brought an end to sin and death. The eternal life in every believer is the life of God, the Zoe life in the absolute, the life as God has it.

Our fellowship is in the apostle's doctrine and the same fellowship they had with the Father and the Son through the Holy Spirit (see John 1:3). All the above was the purpose of the mystery that Paul mentions.

The Promise Is to All the Nations

In your seed all the nations of the earth shall be blessed, because you have obeyed My voice.

Genesis 22:18

This is a Messianic verse. The seed is Jesus, the Messiah. Paul makes this clear in Galatians 3:14-16.

That the blessing of Abraham might come upon the Gentiles in Christ Jesus, that we might receive the promise of the Spirit through faith.

Brethren, I speak in the manner of men: Though it is only a man's covenant, yet if it is confirmed, no one annuls or adds to it. Now to Abraham and his Seed were the promises made. He does not say, "And to seeds," as of many, but as of one, "And to your Seed," who is Christ.

Not seed as of many, but as of one, that one is Christ. Can you see the mystery? Mystery revealed, mystery in purpose, mystery in fellowship.

Again, we see that the blessing is to Abraham and to his seed. Isaac was the son of promise to Abraham and Sara and carried the seed that led to the seed of promise. Through Isaac and Jacob's bloodline, the promised seed came, that is Christ who is the King of nations.

The Manifold Wisdom of God

As we look at verse 10, we learn of the manifold wisdom "to the intent that now the manifold wisdom of God might be made known by the church to the principalities and powers in the heavenly places."

God has a plan. His intent is that His church might know the many-faceted wisdom of God. We have been learning of that wisdom that is from above. Paul is not speaking of some earthly theology school. He is speaking of the kind of wisdom that can only originate in the mind of God and be revealed by the Holy Spirit.

This wisdom begins with what God purposed before He laid the foundation of the earth. That is, Christ is the fullness of His purposes. Christ is begotten of the Father to fulfill David's prophetic word.

> *I will declare the decree:*
> *The LORD has said to Me,*
> *"You are My Son,*
> *Today I have begotten You."*

Psalm 2:7

He also predestined man to the adaption as sons. He did this through Jesus Christ according to His will. He purposed that we should be holy and without blame before Him in love. We learned all this in our first lesson beginning in Ephesians 1.

God's wisdom is rooted in the shedding of blood for the guilty. The blood of one man was sufficient to deal with the sin of all humanity, not just Jews, but of all the nations.

In this manifold wisdom of God, God purposed that all the redeemed of His New Creation would receive the Holy Spirit of the Father and of the Son. He would dwell on the inside of those receiving God's great sacrifice of His Son who was also the promised seed to Abraham.

Certainly, there is more to be said about God's manifold wisdom, but for now, let's lay ahold of these three important facts:

1. God's purpose in Christ
2. Christ's shed blood
3. Christ giving to believers the Holy Spirit who is the Spirit of the Father and the Son.

All three of these dimensions of His wisdom are in the believer which makes up His one holy apostolic church.

- Holy, because He is holy and He has made us holy.

- Apostolic, because He is the Chief Apostle of our faith. Apostle is a sent one. Jesus was sent by the Father for the sins of the whole world. The Father gave to Jesus the twelve men who became the Apostles of the Lamb. They were sent to Israel by Jesus, the Messiah, to preach His Gospel of the Kingdom of God. Paul was called by Jesus to go and preach Christ's Gospel to the Jews first and to the Gentile nations. As we observed in our study, given to Paul and the other apostles was the understanding of the mysteries (see Ephesians 3:3 and 3:8), unsearchable riches of Christ.

- Church, which in Hebrew and Greek means a called-out assembly that governs. The new administration is Christ over all. Ephesians 3:9 (NKJV) uses the word *fellowship* in regard to administrating the mystery which was from the beginning of time. Christ is now administrating His Kingdom purpose through His holy apostolic church revealed by His apostles as the foundation with Christ as the chief cornerstone.

I hope you can see by now what God has in mind through Christ, and that you can see how far removed we have become from what Paul is describing. Can you see with me our need for a move of the Holy Spirit to revive the work of God in our day? The revivals of the past and what we need today is really about bringing the Lord's church back to what these early apostles understood.

Continuing with verse 10:

> *To the intent that now the manifold wisdom of God might be made known by the church to the principalities and powers in the heavenly places.*

We must understand that God's will is to be brought to pass through His church, the body of Christ. As we understand God's purposes and plans, we comprehend how we are to be united in order to fulfill the plan and purpose as one holy body, joined to Christ by the Holy Spirit as one new man on the earth.

It is the church that is meant to demonstrate to the principalities and powers in the heavenly places, God's great mystery—our unity, our holiness, our united understanding of God's plan, and our relationship to God's divine order as a holy nation (see 1 Peter 2:5-9). This is what causes us to be able to defeat the enemy, that is principalities and powers in heavenly places. Our lifestyle as His church is what speaks to the enemies located in heavenly realms.

Our disunity in His church prevents us from fulfilling God's purpose for the church, as Jesus' body unified in the one new man created in Christ Jesus, from defeating the principalities and powers here on earth. The discipling of the nations includes the defeating of those principalities and powers. The discipling of the nations as commanded by our Lord in the Great Commission is the revelation of the manifold wisdom of God in the total defeat of Satan's plans of possessing the nations and controlling humanity. The kingdom of darkness will realize the wisdom of the full intent of God through a unified church, His body, on the last day. It is the church which is His body, that is meant to make the enemies of Christ His footstool. This is what Paul was addressing in 1 Corinthians 15:24-26 when he said:

> *Then comes the end, when He delivers the kingdom to God the Father, when He put an end to all rule and all authority and power. For He must reign till He has put all enemies under His feet. The last enemy that will be destroyed is death.*

Verse 11 says, "according to the eternal purpose, that purpose was fully completed in Christ Jesus our Lord." It is done, but God's plan was for His purpose to be implemented by His church which is His body on the earth.

Verse 12: "In whom we have boldness and access with confidence through faith in Him." Be bold to ask for all the resources of heaven in order to confront the enemy's affronts. We have access to God's throne as we come in faith in Him.

> *Let us therefore come boldly to the throne of grace, that we may obtain mercy and find grace to help in time of need.*
>
> Hebrews 4:16

Verse 13: "Therefore I ask that you do not lose heart at my tribulations for you, which is your glory." Tribulation is an important part of the plan.

> *We must through many tribulations enter the kingdom of God.*
>
> Acts 14:22

What Have We Learned?

1. The purpose of God held within the mystery was that Messiah would unite the human race as the Last Adam the creation of the Holy Spirit.

2. The redeemed Israel would be made up of Jews, Samaritans, and those from all the Gentile nations. Christ's holy apostolic church on the earth. Sent to all the nations with the Good News of Christ's Kingdom.

3. Through the church, the principalities and powers in heavenly places learn of God's plan to redeem humanity and create one new man on the earth to bring the nations to the Lord.

4. Because of all this, we are to have boldness and access to God's power with confidence through faith in Him.

5. Tribulation is a necessary part of this battle.

Ephesians 3:14-21

For this reason I bow my knees to the Father of our Lord Jesus Christ, from whom the whole family in heaven and earth is named, that He would grant you, according to the riches of His glory, to be strengthened with might through His Spirit in the inner man, that Christ may dwell in your hearts through faith; that you, being rooted and grounded in love, may be able to comprehend with all the saints what is the width and length and depth and height—to know the love of Christ which passes knowledge; that you may be filled with all the fullness of God. Now to Him who is able to do exceedingly abundantly above all that we ask or think, according to the power that works in us, to Him be glory in the church by Christ Jesus to all generations, forever and ever. Amen.

Application Of the Mystery

We have seen the revealing of the mystery, the purpose of the mystery, and the fellowship of the mystery. Now let's consider the application of the mystery. Beginning with verse 14, Paul reveals his personal appreciation for what God has shown him to pass on to others. He humbles himself before God through bended knees. Paul is taking a posture of humility as we all should when we realize the magnitude of what God has done and is revealing to us.

Notice how personal and intimate Paul gets in his demonstration of honor and gratitude as he recognizes the Father of our Lord Jesus Christ. I have already mentioned Jesus' faithfulness to His house. It is the house that the Father has given to Jesus. His church is part of that house. All that God is doing is connected to the mystery, the one new man made up of both Jews and Gentiles. The Gentiles are also made up of the many nations. Included in the many are "all nations, tribes, peoples and tongues" (see Revelation 7:9-10). All these are being brought into God's glorious family. Indeed, "Salvation belongs to our God who sits on the throne, and to the Lamb!" Paul is speaking of one family coming out of all the families on the earth. Consider verses 15-16: "from whom the whole family in heaven and earth is named, that He would grant you, according to the riches of His glory, to be strengthened with might through His Spirit in the inner man,"

It is first the inner man that needs attention. He is neglected many times because our flesh demands so much attention. The Jewish contention was over the flesh wanting recognition. Many of our divisions in the church today are principally over the flesh demanding what it wants. This is what Paul was addressing in the Corinthian Church.

> *But the natural man does not receive the things of the Spirit of God, for they are foolishness to him; nor can he know them, because they are spiritually discerned.*

> 1 Corinthians 2:14

It would be worth the time to study the first two chapters of 1 Corinthians because there Paul sorts out the issues of the flesh and the spirit in the context of the church.

Riches Of His Glory

Back to Ephesians 3, we find Paul on his knees in prayer for these Ephesian believers. He is praying that God would grant them "according to the riches of His glory." God's glory. What are the riches of His glory? It is the mystery of which we have been speaking—that which was hidden to all before Christ's appearing and before His resurrection from the dead. It is the new life in Christ. It is His resurrection power that becomes infused in the believer by faith in all that Christ has accomplished. It is what Paul says next: "To be strengthened with might through His Spirit in the inner man."

When we are born again, it is our spirit man that is regenerated. Not our soul, but our spirit. Our spirit was part of the natural aspect of our life. It was human, it was natural, and it was without eternal life sustenance. Through the Holy Spirit of God, our spirit is born again. It is regenerated. It has eternal life in its being. It contains the seed of God's word made alive. This is what Peter was addressing when he says:

Having been born again, not of corruptible seed but incorruptible, through the word of God which lives and abides forever, because

"All flesh is as grass,
And all the glory of man as the flower of the grass.
The grass withers,
And its flower falls away,
But the word of the Lord endures forever."

Now this is the word which by the gospel was preached to you.

1 Peter 1:23-25

If our soul hopes to learn and develop in the things of the Spirit, our inner man must first receive. Our inner man must be strengthened with might; that might comes from the Holy Spirit.

Paul goes on to ask in prayer articulated in verse 17, "that Christ may dwell in your hearts through faith." Remember, the writer of Hebrews says:

But without faith it is impossible to please Him, for he who comes to God must believe that He is, and that He is a rewarder of those who diligently seek Him.

Hebrews 11:6

Remember also what we learned in Ephesians 2:8, "For by grace you have been saved through faith, and that not of yourselves; it is the gift of God." It is not our natural faith, but a gift of faith given by God through the Holy Spirit, that causes our spirit (or inner man) to be made alive and strengthened daily.

When Jesus is dwelling or reigning in our hearts through faith, all contention stops. He has the last word. And that last word is *love*! We are to be rooted and grounded in love. He is love and expects His love to be established in our inner man and find the life of love living out through us. In other words, His love, which begins in one's spirit or inner man, is meant to change our thinking so we can communicate the love and life of God in Christ through the power of His Holy Spirit!

In verse 18, Paul focuses on what God's intended plan is when he speaks about being rooted and grounded in love so that we may be able to comprehend with all the saints what is the width and length and depth and height. Remember, Paul is writing and praying from his prison cell. What a prayer he prays, not only for these Ephesian believers but for all the saints! You are included in this prayer. It is God who made Paul's words eternal.

Let us pray this prayer for ourselves and for others. "That we might be able to comprehend." There is much that comes against us. Much that is intended to hinder our faith and forward motion in God's Kingdom. Without spiritual comprehension, we cannot move forward in God. Remember, we are learning through our study how important the spirit of revelation is in our ability to know and comprehend the things of the Spirit of God.

This comprehension is for all saints. Say, "That is me!" God's desire is for His corporate body. Remember, we are one new man in Christ Jesus. The expression, "What is the width and length and depth and height," speaks to the totality of God's purpose in Christ. This picture is given to us prophetically in Revelation 21:2 as we see the holy city, "New Jerusalem, coming down out of heaven from God, prepared as a bride adorned for her husband." New Jerusalem is the bride of Christ, His church prepared for her husband.

We must quit thinking only with our natural minds. We must see by the Spirit if we are to embrace what Paul is praying for us to understand. Look how Paul connects his request to the love of God in verse 19. "To know the love of Christ which passes knowledge; that you may be filled with all the fullness of God." What an incredible statement to know Christ's love which cannot be known. It cannot be figured out intellectually or with human reasoning. It is only by the Holy Spirit this can be known and experienced. We are called to enter into worship and relationship that is meant to grow into a "fullness of God."

> *Now to Him who is able to do exceedingly abundantly above all that we ask or think, according to the power that works in us, to Him be glory in the church by Christ Jesus to all generations, forever and ever. Amen.*

> Ephesians 3:20-21

God's plan has always been to use His creation man to accomplish His purposes on the earth. Part of the plan is that man intercedes for God's work to be accomplished on the earth among the nations. The Father wants us relationally involved with His awesome plan. It is not like a servant, but a son who does his father's bidding.

The exceedingly abundantly above all that we ask or think is more about our calling to do His will than it is about every little thing we want to be done. His power is working in us to do His will and to advance His kingdom plan. He gets the glory and that glory is in the church. It is by Christ Jesus to all generations.

God's view is eternal, not just an immediate or momentary need. Again, consider Paul in a Roman jail. In his mind, he was Christ's prisoner for the sake of the saints. We are part of God's work forever and ever. Amen.

What Have We Learned?

1. There is an application of the mystery. His church is His house made up of all the nations of the earth.

2. This work of God in our life has its beginnings in the inner man.

3. The work of God is a work of faith operating in our spirit man.

4. God wants us to be able to comprehend with all the saints the width, and length and depth and height.

5. God wants us to know the love of Christ which passes all knowledge.

6. God wants us to be filled with all the fullness of God.

7. He is able to do exceedingly abundantly above all we ask or think.

Chapter 4

Ephesians 4:1-6

I, therefore, the prisoner of the Lord, beseech you to walk worthy of the calling with which you were called, with all lowliness and gentleness, with longsuffering, bearing with one another in love, endeavoring to keep the unity of the Spirit in the bond of peace. There is one body and one Spirit, just as you were called in one hope of your calling; one Lord, one faith, one baptism; one God and Father of all, who is above all, and through all, and in you all.

Prisoner of The Lord

Paul, God's apostle to the Gentile believers, continues to develop his premise of what God intended in the beginning and is now being revealed and worked out because of Christ Jesus and His life. Remember how Paul ended chapter 3 as he declared:

> *Now to Him who is able to do exceedingly abundantly above all that we ask or think, according to the power that works in us, to Him be glory in the church by Christ Jesus to all generations, forever and ever. Amen.*

> Ephesians 3:21-22

What God is using Paul to birth, is happening in a Roman prison. It is happening in the crucible of suffering and absolute surrender to Christ and His will! From that position, Paul beseeches us to walk worthy of the calling with which we have been called. We are not just saved from our sins, but called to a life that demonstrates God's redemptive work in our heart and through our lifestyle. Paul goes on to show us what that looks like. Paul is the model of what redemptive grace looks like in a life well lived as "the prisoner of the Lord."

The Measurement of a Life Surrendered

Paul gives us words that express what a surrendered life looks like. Let us examine the measurement of a life surrendered to God's will.

First, we see a life of lowliness or humility. Humility is a lifestyle that puts others before oneself. One of the best books ever written on the subject of humility is Andrew Murry's little book entitled *Humility*. Humility is seen in God's response through Jesus to His fallen man.

Second, is our need to humble ourselves before God and receive His saving grace to be able to return to a right standing before God.

In the third aspect of humility, we have the mystery of grace, which teaches us that as we lose ourselves in the overwhelming greatness of redeeming love, humility becomes to us the consummation of everlasting blessedness and adoration.

Following humility is gentleness. Many times, gentleness is a true demonstration of humility. They work hand in hand with one another. I believe that the movie, *A Beautiful Day in the Neighborhood*, about the friendship between Mister Rogers (Fred Rogers) and a journalist, Tom Junod, is a beautiful testimony about both humility and gentleness. A must-see!

Following gentleness, Paul mentions longsuffering. Longsuffering is the act of bearing with others when they might not be giving the same kind of caring attitude to us. It is to love others who are broken, demonstrating anger and bad attitudes, especially when it is toward you. Paul instructs us to bear with one another with love.

Next, Paul tells us to "endeavor" to keep the unity of the Spirit in the bond of peace. This kind of lifestyle will require prayer, daily looking into the scriptures and complete dependence upon the Holy

Spirit. You can see that Paul is calling all of us to a life fully dependent on the Power of the Holy Spirit. God does not expect you or me to live this kind of lifestyle without His Holy Spirit's life living out through us.

> *There is one body and one Spirit, just as you were*
> *called in one hope of your calling; one Lord, one faith,*
> *one baptism; one God and Father of all, who is above*
> *all, and through all, and in you all.*

> Ephesians 4:4-6

Consider how the one new man is revealed here in this sentence. It is about a body, His body, made up of many members. The Spirit of God is One Holy Spirit. He is not divided, but the same Spirit that raised Jesus from the dead is alive in you and in me. We are all called into the same hope. There is no diversity of hope. It is one hope. That hope is connected to the same calling. The calling is to His life lived out in us. The fruit of the Spirit is given to each believer. It is not diverse but is fully mature and lived out through God's power. Our calling is the same when it comes to His life being manifested in and through us.

There is only one Lord. His nature is the same in each believer. Not everything that is called Christian is indeed Christian or Christ-like. His nature does not change from person to person. This is not about personality but about Christ our one Lord. The issue is maturity! Not everyone is living out the Christ like-life at the same maturity level. This is why, within the body of Christ, all the above is required, beginning with humility.

It is not many faiths, but one faith. The standard is the scriptures and the power is His Holy Spirit. Remember that together we are called as one new man. There is no boredom in humility, there is no boredom in gentleness, and there is no boredom in longsuffering. And there certainly is no boredom in love.

Our identity is in one baptism, His baptism, the baptism of His death and the resurrection of His life. This is at the core of our divisions. You're not baptized to a church, a denomination, a set of rules, a system of doctrine, but to a person, the person of the Lord Jesus Christ. You are connected to His death. And you are joined to His resurrection. You have become a new creation through the Lord Jesus Christ.

> *Therefore, if anyone is in Christ, he is a new creation; old things have passed away; behold all things have become new.*

2 Corinthians 5:17

One of our greatest problems in the Christian church is the matter of identity. Paul called it carnality in 1 Corinthians 1:10-17. We identify with so many individuals and structures with such a variety of private doctrine, rather than Christ and Christ alone through the power of the Holy Spirit.

Verse 6, "One God and Father of all, who is above all, and through all, and in you all."

We come to the greatest mystery of all. The mystery begins with one God and Father of all. There is only one true God and He is a Father by His very being. He is God and Father of Adam. In Luke 3:38, He is called God and Father of our Lord Jesus Christ. He is our Father, "Who art in heaven." He is the Father of the fatherless. Our God and Father is above all. There is no one higher. He is through all. That is, He is Spirit, He is not material that was created, but He is eternal. And He is in you all. Our God, the Eternal One also lives within all who receive His love through Jesus Christ.

What Have We Learned?

1. Through Paul, we learn what a fully surrendered life looks like.

2. Humility: God's response to His fallen creation man; our need to humble ourselves in receiving God's love; the mystery of grace that teaches us of losing our self in His redeeming love.

3. Gentleness: the true demonstration of humility.

4. Longsuffering: bearing with others when they are not giving the same kind of response.

5. Endeavoring to keep the unity of the Spirit in the bond of peace.

6. One body and one Spirit, one new man.

7. Identity in His death and power in His resurrection.

8. The One God and Father of all.

Ephesians 4:7-10

But to each one of us grace was given according to the measure of Christ's gift. Therefore He says:

> *When He ascended on high,*
> *He led captivity captive,*
> *And gave gifts to men."*

(Now this, "He ascended"—what does it mean but that He also first descended into the lower parts of the earth? He who descended is also the One who ascended far above all the heavens, that He might fill all things.)

Purpose And Calling

Verse 7: "But to each one of us grace was given according to the measure of Christ's gift." Every saint of God has been given grace. Yes, certainly saving grace, but saving grace is not what Paul is referring to here. This grace has to do with our purpose and calling. It speaks to gifts given by Jesus of His life in order to do God's will. Those gifts are given in "measure." In other words, there are different strengths and sizes of these gifts. Not everyone has the same level of anointing.

We all have a sphere of influence in which we move. My own experience began when I received Christ into my life in 1957. Over the next years, as I grew in Christ, I received a call to preach in 1960. I began to have grace to lead in the youth ministry and in my relationships in high school. Some lives were influenced by my life to give their life to Christ. When I went to college, that grace developed into influence in the church and outside my own denomination.

As I grew in my knowledge of the Word of God, I received leadership opportunities that helped develop my future pastoral call. One of those opportunities was to teach in a local bible college. The

Spirit of the Lord was increasing the teaching gift. He was also giving me a vision for the larger church and not just my local church. Over the next 10 years, I went through a deep pruning in my life and ministry. It could have totally taken me out, but God was faithful and I came through this difficult time with much experience that has served me well.

As the Lord moved me to my next assignment, I experienced a tremendous increase of the measure of Christ's gifts in my life. The Lord increased my sphere of influence from a local church and a local Bible college to a citywide ministry and an international outreach to the nations.

As I review my life in Christ, I would have never been able to do what the Lord has allowed without the "measure of the grace of Christ." All the glory goes to Him!

I suggest you also consider your life from the point of your redemption and conversion to the present. See if you can recognize Christ's measure of grace that He has given to you. How has He used you and what burdens has He given to you? What gifts can you recognize have come from the Lord and how have those gifts been a blessing to others?

Verse 8 identifies what happened when Christ ascended: "When He ascended on high, He led captivity captive, and gave gifts to men."

The first thing Jesus did was for those righteous dead waiting for Messiah's day. He led those who had been captive in upper sheol (or paradise or the bosom of Abraham) and led them out of where they had been waiting, into a captivity of His grace. Consider two scripture references. In Luke 16:22, the beggar who had died was carried to Abraham's Bosom. And in Luke 23:43, the thief on the cross asked Jesus to remember him when He came into His kingdom. That beggar went to Paradise with Christ that day. He arose with all the righteous awaiting their day of release. Then in Heaven, from His throne, He gives gifts to men. All of the gifts of God come to mankind as the grace or favor of our great King.

Verse 9: Paul explains that before Christ ascended, "He also first descended into the lower parts of the earth." In His descent, He did more than just empty paradise, He descended to the "lowest parts of the earth"—hades itself.

> *I am He who lives, and was dead, and behold, I am alive forevermore. Amen. And I have the keys of Hades and of Death.*
>
> Revelation 1:18

Jesus took from the devil the "keys of Hades and of Death." Our King now possesses those keys. What a picture of the fullness of what Christ has accomplished on our behalf.

Verse 10: "He who descended is also the One who ascended far above all the heavens, that He might fill all things."

This perhaps is the clearest statement of what our great God and King has accomplished. Only by the Holy Spirit can we truly understand the fullness of Christ's great redemptive work. Indeed, as Jesus said from His cross: "It is finished."

I mentioned before that chapter 4 is about government. Can you see how completely Christ has overcome and is presently reigning from heaven as God's appointed Messiah King who is filling all things? There are many who are waiting for Jesus to finish the work. I say No! The work is done already. He is waiting for us to understand how totally and completely He has finished His part and now it is the church's responsibility to clean up the mess on planet earth.

Remember what Jesus told the five hundred before He ascended to His throne of glory:

> *And Jesus came and spoke to them, saying, All authority has been given to Me in heaven and on earth.*

Go therefore and make disciples of all the nations, baptizing them in the name of the Father and of the Son and of the Holy Spirit, teaching them to observe all things that I have commanded you; and lo, I am with you always, even to the end of the age. Amen.

Matthew 28:18-20

What Have We Learned?

1. We are all included in Christ's work on earth. Each one has received grace to partner with Jesus in the great work of His Kingdom purpose. He gives to each, a gift, in order to fulfill our individual purpose.

2. We all have a sphere to influence for the Gospel of our Lord's Kingdom.

3. The gift we are given begins as a seed and grows as we grow in Him. The gift is given as a measure. None of us have everything. He has meant for us to work together as one body.

4. We learned how Christ Jesus delivered captives from upper sheol in His resurrection and ascension.

5. We learned that He ascended far above all the heavens to fill all things.

6. We have begun to see the government of God which has been established in Messiah's present reign.

Next, we will learn about the Lord's fivefold ministry graces that are given to govern His kingdom purposes on the earth through His church.

105

Ephesians 4:11-16

And He Himself gave some to be apostles, some prophets, some evangelists, and some pastors and teachers, for the equipping of the saints for the work of ministry, for the edifying of the body of Christ, till we all come to the unity of the faith and of the knowledge of the Son of God, to a perfect man, to the measure of the stature of the fullness of Christ; that we should no longer be children, tossed to and fro and carried about with every wind of doctrine, by the trickery of men, in the cunning craftiness of deceitful plotting, but, speaking the truth in love, may grow up in all things into Him who is the head—Christ—from whom the whole body, joined and knit together by what every joint supplies, according to the effective working by which every part does its share, causes growth of the body for the edifying of itself in love.

It is important to understand the difference between the Twelve Apostles of the Lamb and what we are about to study in Ephesians 4:11. Those original apostles were given to Jesus by the Father, (see John 17:6). Those men are distinct and have a place that no other New Testament apostles possess. In Matthew 19:28, Jesus said to them that in the regeneration they would sit upon twelve thrones and judge the twelve tribes of Israel. Their word continues to judge the Lord's people today. Revelation 21:14 identifies those twelve as *"Apostles of the Lamb."* The apostles that are referenced in Ephesians 4:11, I call "the ascension gift apostles" because they came after the other twelve. Paul is an archetype of those apostles and is a bridge between the original twelve and those who followed, including modern day apostles.

Five-Fold:

Verse 11 reveals the five-fold ascension gifts that Christ has given to His church. These gifts or graces were given by Jesus to His Church

106

for the purpose of administrating His government on earth. Jesus is giving of Himself by the Holy Spirit to members of His body. Each gift is found in the Lord's life and ministry while He ministered on earth.

Remember that Jesus told His disciples that all power in heaven and in earth had been given to Him. Jesus was seated on heavens throne and, from there, He gave gifts, ministry to men. He gave of His own ministry anointing. He is the Apostle, He is the Prophet, He is the Evangelist, He is the Pastor or Shepherd, and He is the Teacher.

Jesus was sent by the Father; thus, He is the "Apostle" sent from the Father's throne. Jesus was "that Prophet" whom Moses said would come (see Deuteronomy 18:18-19). He summed up all that the OT prophets prophesied concerning the Messiah. Jesus was the "Evangel" of "good news" personified. He reached out further than any other. Jesus is the "Chief Shepherd of the flock." Ephesians 4:11 is the only place in the New Testament that the word "pastor" is used. A better word would have been "shepherd" as used elsewhere in the New Testament writings. Jesus is the "Teacher of teachers." He not only brought the "Word of God," He is the "Logos" or "the Living Word of God."

Each of these ministries is known as the "Ascension Gift Ministries" of Jesus Christ and His Kingdom. He gave these gifts to His church for the administrating of His Body. These gifts are part of the "Keys of the Kingdom" which Jesus spoke of in Matthew 16:18. In Jesus' death, burial, and resurrection, He gave to His redeemed Israel a new administration. No longer was there a "tribe of priests," but now a kingdom of priests called from all the nations to be His redeemed holy nation in the earth. The Spirit of God began to bring forth "a holy apostolic church." A people sent by our Lord, first to "natural Israel" through the command of repentance and then to the nations, also being called to repentance (Acts 17:30-31). The Spirit began creating "One" holy people throughout the earth.

The "apostolic gift" spoken about here in Ephesians 4:11 is different than that of the original apostles. Those original apostles were a gift from the Father to Jesus (John 17:6). Paul speaks of himself as "one born out of due time" (1 Corinthians 15:8).

He speaks of his gift as "grace given to him for the Gentiles" (Ephesians 3:2). I call those original apostles, the "Apostles of the Lamb." There will never again be apostles that have the same apostolic call as those men who were given to Christ Jesus by the Father. They were the eyewitnesses of His miracles and His teachings. They were eyewitnesses of His crucifixion and His resurrection. They laid the foundation for His church, establishing Jesus Christ as the "cornerstone" of the Temple that the Lord Himself was building as promised to David in 2 Samuel 7:13. Those Apostles and the word of the Prophets spoken throughout the Old Testament became the foundation of this House that the Lord was building.

The apostles mentioned in Ephesians 4:11 are what I call, "ascension gift apostles." They were called and given to the body of Christ from Jesus when He was seated on His throne at the right hand of the Father. They received the "word of the original apostles." They are called and sent to the nations bringing the message of "repentance" and the messages of Christ present reign over the nations of the earth.

The "prophets" mentioned here are New Testament Prophets which prophesy vision for God's people. There are examples of New Testament prophets in the book of Acts. The New Testament teaches that God's will is that all His people would "prophesy" (see 1 Corinthians 14:5, 29-33).

The "evangelists" carries the "Good News of the Kingdom of God to many people. He calls men and women to repentance. Usually, power gifts accompany the gift of the Evangelist. He does not stay in one place, but travels from place to place sharing the good news. Please read Acts 6 – 8 for a good picture of the ministry of the Evangelist in the life of Philip.

The "pastor" is the most familiar of the gifts to most Christians. The word *pastor* does not communicate the true meaning of government placement. Throughout the New Testament, the title of "elder," "overseer," "shepherd," and "bishop" are used to describe this gift mentioned in Ephesians 4:11. Each word has a similar meaning as translated from the Greek or Septuagint manuscripts. They all carry the thought of "government." Here is what Vines Greek Expository Dictionary of New Testament words have to say:

VINES: poimen (poimh/n, NT:4166), "a shepherd, one who tends herds or flocks" (not merely one who feeds them), is used metaphorically of Christian "pastors," Eph 4:11. "Pastors" guide as well as feed the flock, cf. Acts 20:28, which with v. 17, indicates that this was the service committed to elders (overseers or bishops); so also in 1 Peter 5:1,2, "tend the flock... exercising the oversight," RV; this involves tender care and vigilant superintendence. See SHEPHERD. Metaphorically of those who act as pastors in the churches, Eph 4:11.

1. presbuteros (presbu/tero, an adjective, the comparative degree of *presbus*, "an old man, an elder,"

Matt 16:21; 26:47; thirdly, those who managed public affairs in the various cities, Luke 7:3; (3) in the Christian churches those who, being raised up and qualified by the work of the Holy Spirit, were appointed to have the spiritual care of, and to exercise oversight over, the churches. To these the term "bishops," *episkopoi*, or "overseers," is applied (see Acts 20, v. 17 with v. 28, and Titus 1:5 and 7), the latter term indicating the nature of their work *presbuteroi* their maturity of spiritual experience. The divine arrangement seen throughout the NT was for a plurality of these to be appointed in each church, Acts 14:23; 20:17; Phil 1:1; 1 Tim 5:17; Titus 1:5. The duty of "elders" is described by the verb *episkopeo*. They were appointed according as they had given evidence of fulfilling the divine qualifications, Titus 1:6 to 9; cf. 1 Tim 3:1-7 and 1 Peter 5:2;

The "teachers" are those who have revelation and understanding to teach God's word to the church at large. These teachers are a gift from the Lord to His Church. The teaching gift is found in the other four gifts mentioned here as well.

Let's be clear: these fivefold gifts given by the Lord Jesus to His church are not soulish or accomplished by natural means, like going to a Bible school or seminary. One may have gone to Bible school or seminary, but this does not make one an apostle, or prophet, or evangelists, or pastor, or teacher. Only the Holy Spirit, by the direction of Christ, can truly call a person to one of these offices or gifts. These are not "titles," they are charis or gifts given by Christ to the benefit of His church!

VINES: charisma (xa/risma, NT:5486), "a gift of grace, a gift involving grace" (charis) on the part of God as the donor, is used (a) of His free bestowments upon sinners, Rom 5:15,16; 6:23; 11:29; (b) of His endowments upon believers by the operation of the Holy Spirit in the churches, Rom 12:6; 1 Cor 1:7; 12:4,9,28,30,31; 1 Tim 4:14; 2 Tim 1:6; 1 Peter 4:10; (c) of that which is imparted through human instruction, Rom 1:11; (d) of the natural "gift" of continence, consequent upon the grace of God as Creator, 1 Cor 7:7; (e) of gracious deliverances granted in answer to the prayers of fellow believers, 2 Cor 1:11.

Next, we will pick up at verse 12 and speak of the necessity of these gifts in Christ's Body. Equipping, edifying, unity of the faith and the knowledge of the Son of God can only come through these appointed grace gifts given by Jesus to His church.

What Have We Learned?

1. Jesus—the resurrected Christ—is the giver of these five ascension gifts of the Spirit to His body.

2. These gifts speak to the government of Christ's kingdom.

3. We learned that these five ministry gifts are seen in the life of Jesus through His human ministry.

4. These gifts are given in measure according to Christ calling on a life.

5. We learned about all 5 of these gifts. We spent the most time speaking about the "apostolic" and "pastoral" gifts which carry the most weight of the government of God within their office. Let's be clear, these "fivefold gifts" given by the Lord Jesus to His church are not "soulish" or accomplished by natural means, like going to a Bible School or Seminary. One may have gone to Bible School or Seminary, but this does not make one an apostle, or prophet, or evangelists, or pastor, or teacher. Only the Holy Spirit by the direction of Christ can truly call a person to one of these offices or gifts. These are not "titles." They are Charis or gifts given by Christ to the benefit of His church!

Equipping

Verse 12 begins to unfold the purpose of the five ascension gifts. These gifts are given to the body of Christ for the purpose of equipping the saints for the work of ministry and the edifying of the body of Christ—equipping or making us ready for the work we have been given to do. Recall what we discussed in chapter 2 concerning our work for the Lord. We saw how the Lord had prepared us for good works.

> *For we are His workmanship, created in Christ Jesus*
> *for good works, which God prepared beforehand that*
> *we should walk in them.*

Ephesians 2:10

All the saints are called to the "good work" of the kingdom and not just a select few! We all have an assignment. Part of the excitement is to seek the Lord and learn what He has called us to do personally in extending His kingdom here on earth. We are all called; we all have work to do. And each of us has a sphere to touch in people's lives.

Those who are called into the fivefold grace mentioned in verse 11 have the assignment of equipping all of God's people for ministry. Ministry is not a profession, but a calling. It is a calling to serve the Lord, but also to serve others through His imparted life. All saints have been called to ministry and all need to be equipped for the work.

Some examples may be:

- A Christian businessman needs to see his business as an opportunity to extend the kingdom of God.

- A Christian student needs to see how he or she may influence their campus for Christ.

- A parent needs to help their son or daughter find their calling in Christ within the mountains of culture in which they live.

We should all experience an equipping which brings edification to others, first within Christ's body and then outward to the world around us. This could include:

- Being equipped to pray for individuals, church leadership, the lost, and government leaders (see 1Timothy 2 and Romans 13:1-7).

- Learning how to understand God's Word and how to apply the Word of God in our life. Being equipped in the prophetic in order to: edify, exhort, and comfort (see 1Corinthians 14:3 and 31).

- Learning to discern what is happening in the spiritual realm around us (see 1 John 18-20).

- Learning to lead people into a relationship with Christ, baptism, and becoming part of a local body of believers so they also can be equipped.

And so much more that I could list. I am sure that you can see this is work, the work of the ministry—the beautiful service of the Lord's kingdom work in spreading the gospel and seeing the kingdom of God increased.

The next thing we learn is about the goal of the edifying of the body of Christ. We are all used to edify one another.

> *Till we all come to the unity of the faith and of the knowledge of the Son of God, to a perfect man, to the measure of the stature of the fullness of Christ.*

> Ephesians 4:13

This can be a scripture that is difficult to get our heads around because it is so large in its purpose and we are so aware of our own limitations. Remember what Paul said in Ephesians.

> *Now to Him who is able to do far more abundantly beyond all that we ask or think, according to the power that works within us.*

> Ephesians 3:20

Obviously, verse 13 is referring to the completed work of the Holy Spirit in our lives. At least we know the goal and the expectant end result that God is working in His church.

> *That we should no longer be children, tossed to and fro and carried about with every wind of doctrine, by the trickery of men, in the cunning craftiness of deceitful plotting, but, speaking the truth in love, may grow up in all things into Him who is the head—Chris—from whom the whole body, joined and knit together by what every joint supplies, according to the effective working by which every part does its share, causes growth of the body for the edifying of itself in love.*

> Ephesians 4:14-16

These verses should be realized now! The maturity should be manifesting in our life presently. This means learning to grow up into Christ. That is, being well established in the Word of Christ. There are many winds of doctrine that are here today and gone tomorrow. There is trickery, cunning craftiness and deceitful plotting of men that use the faith for their own soulish and sometimes evil intentions.

When we begin to have more concern for others who are in need than ourselves, we have begun to enter into what Paul is sharing in verse 15. Love is the critical component!

Verse 16 caps it for us, "The whole body is joined together by what every joint supplies." The fact is, every believer is important and every believer has a part to contribute. It is the evil one, the devil who seeks to trick us into believing that we do not really matter. Others do, but we don't. The big lie!

What Have We Learned?

1.   Charisma, or gift, is really God's grace and favor.

2.   The Lord equips us for all we are called to do. The Holy Spirit supplies gifts through us, which are used to assist us in ministering to the needs of others.

3.   The fivefold gifts are given to the body for its equipping to do the work of ministry and to edify the body of Christ. Those ministries are not personal possession but gifting's to help others do the work of ministry.

4.   The gifts mentioned here are meant to help us be unified in the faith. They are given to the body to help us in the knowledge of the Son of God. The gifts are given to help us become mature, to the measure of the stature of the fullness of Christ.

5.   We learned that these gifts are given to protect us from the trickery of men. They are given to help us speak the truth in love.

6. Ultimately the gifts cause growth of the body for the edifying of itself in love.

We need to ask ourselves, "How are we doing?"

Love Of God in His Body Is on The Move

Verse 14, "We should no longer be children." A foundation truth is more than conversion. It is also maturity or growing up as sons and daughters of God. It is not to remain a child, but to become a son or daughter with knowledge and understanding in the family of God. Jesus came as a baby, empty-headed, needing to learn from the holy scriptures who He is and what He had come to do (see Philippians 2). "And Jesus increased in wisdom and stature, and in favor with God and man" (Luke 2:52).

Here are a few scriptures on growth for us to consider:

- 2 Peter 3:18: "But grow in the grace and knowledge of our Lord and Savior Jesus Christ."

- 2 Thessalonians 1:3: The Thessalonians grew exceedingly in faith.

- Philippians 1:9: Paul prayed for their love to abound more and more.

- 1 Peter 2:2: "Desire the pure milk of the word, that you may grow thereby."

Growing Up

Some people seem to like staying spiritual babies. They don't want to grow up. It's easy to be a baby. No responsibility while others feed you, clothe you and change your diaper. In the church, you don't have to teach, rebuke sin, or do the work of ministry. It's a free ride! Today, many are consumers rather than givers.

Yet being a baby is not the goal of life. We are born babies so we can grow up and be productive and useful. Likewise, we are born again so we can become mature Christians, actively serving the Lord and His eternal purpose.

One of the conditions for becoming a child of God is repentance. One must determine to turn from sin and go to work in God's vineyard. Then one must bring forth the fruits of repentance. This will lead us to grow and improve in God's work. Otherwise, we have not accomplished our purpose for becoming children of God.

> *For this you were called, because Christ also suffered for us, leaving us an example, that you should follow His steps.*
>
> 1 Peter 2:21

Jesus set an example for us, which we should follow in His steps. We should ask ourselves, "Don't I want to grow up to be spiritually strong like Jesus?"

Part of the process of growing up is found in the study of God's Word.

> *But you must continue in the things which you have learned and been assured of, knowing from whom you have learned them, and that from childhood you have known the Holy Scriptures, which are able to make you wise for salvation through faith which is in Christ Jesus.*
>
> *All Scripture is given by inspiration of God, and is profitable for doctrine, for reproof, for correction, for instruction in righteousness, that the man of God may be complete, thoroughly equipped for every good work.*
>
> 2 Timothy 3:14-17

Timothy first learned from his family as a child. He was taught a reverence for the Holy Scriptures because the scriptures were held in high regard. He came to learn that the scriptures were able to make him wise concerning his need of salvation. He developed faith through the scriptures, and that faith pointed him to Christ Jesus. Timothy continued to learn from a spiritual father, Paul. Timothy became grounded in apostolic revelation and truth as he continued to grow as a man who is complete, thoroughly equipped to do every good work.

In 2,000 years of church history, many winds of doctrine have been produced, but God has been restoring understanding to His people through true apostolic teaching. Only what the apostles understood by the revelation of the Holy Spirit through God's grace given them will produce Christ-like maturity and the eternal work of the kingdom of God.

Verse 15 is the necessary and absolute evidence of Christ-likeness: speaking the truth in love. This is the goal of maturity. This is growing up in all things into Him who is the head—Christ. This reveals our maturity in Christ. Even as they were crucifying the Son of God, He cried out: "Father, forgive them, for they do not know what they do" (Luke 23:34).

Verse 15 leads beautifully into verse 16:

> *From whom the whole body, joined and knit together*
> *by what every joint supplies, according to the effective*
> *working by which every part does its share, causes*
> *growth of the body for the edifying of itself in love.*

We deal too much with individualism and not enough with the corporate body of Christ and how we treat one another! Individually, we all have responsibilities. It begins with our service in the body and to Christ's body. The body of Christ by its unity and love serves the Lord in His outreach to the world. There is no other apostolic view. Paul nails it here. This is the reason all these gifts are needed. It is to build up the Lord's body by edifying itself in love.

The truths we have been studying in this writing are critical to our walk with the Lord and with one another. They are also critical to our reaching the nations with the life-changing, good news of Christ's kingdom—His kingdom revealed in His church, motivated by love. A love demonstrated towards one another and then out word to the world. By love which came from heaven to transform the world through a living, breathing corporate body.

What Did We Learn in Our Last Teaching Time?

1. We are no longer children. We begin as a child with the goal of growing up into Christ together as the body of Christ.

2. We have a responsibility before Christ our head and toward one another as members of His body.

3. Truth and love go hand in hand. If you speak the truth but do not demonstrate the love, you missed God's plan and others might miss it too.

4. Part of the process of growing up into Christ comes from the study of God's Word.

5. God's view is toward the whole body being joined and knit together by what is supplied by each one toward one another.

6. We must move from individualism toward body life if we are to fulfill God's plan on planet earth.

7. Live in the world by love demonstrated towards one another and then outward to the world by love which came from heaven to transform the world through a living, breathing corporate body.

Ephesians 4:17-24

This I say, therefore, and testify in the Lord, that you should no longer walk as the rest of the Gentiles walk, in the futility of their mind, having their understanding darkened, being alienated from the life of God, because of the ignorance that is in them, because of the blindness of their heart; who, being past feeling, have given themselves over to lewdness, to work all uncleanness with greediness. But you have not so learned Christ, if indeed you have heard Him and have been taught by Him, as the truth is in Jesus: that you put off, concerning your former conduct, the old man which grows corrupt according to the deceitful lusts, and be renewed in the spirit of your mind, and that you put on the new man which was created according to God, in true righteousness and holiness.

Old Versus New

This passage is a powerful exhortation, teaching, and wonderful picture of the contrast between the old man nature and the new man nature. Let's break this down into smaller pieces that we can pray over and meditate upon.

Once again, Paul connects what he is saying to his previous teaching, summed up in one new man. What follows here comes from Paul's understanding, but also, he is representing the Lord and His will for us, "That you should no longer walk as the rest of the Gentiles walk, in the futility of their mind."

Futility, by definition, means "pointlessness or uselessness." Have you noticed that much of the world's conversation is just that? It is filled with opinions, distortions, and many times it is just plain pointless. I must admit, I personally put up with it because I want to build relationship so maybe I can share the point of it all which is Christ. Jesus led the way. Listen to what He told His own disciples.

> *He answered him and said, 'O faithless generation, how long shall I be with you? How long shall I bear with you? Bring him to Me.' Then they brought him to Him. And when he saw Him, immediately the spirit convulsed him, and he fell on the ground and wallowed, foaming at the mouth.*

> Mark 9:19-20

Verse 18: "Having their understanding darkened, being alienated from the life of God, because of the ignorance that is in them, because of the blindness of their heart."

Understanding darkened. Most have their understanding darkened because they just do not know or others have robbed them of what they did know in part. Many struggle in sharing their faith because they constantly come up against this struggle of the mind. The world has its viewpoints based upon limited or no understanding of God's plan and His principles of life. Consider what Paul told the Roman believers:

> *Although they knew God, they did not glorify Him as God, nor were thankful, but became futile in their thoughts, and their foolish hearts were darkened.*

> Romans 1:21

The second point that Paul makes is that the Gentiles or nations are alienated from the life of God. Natural Israel had that life through the covenant God made with Abraham and obedience to the Law given to Moses. The covenant life promise was fulfilled in Christ. The message of God's life gift was also made available to the Gentiles through faith in Christ. These Ephesian Christians were once alienated from this life but now have come into the life of Christ through grace working by faith.

Through the fall and the growing rebellion in mankind, the Gentiles became ignorant of God's Life. Paul identifies the deeper issue of the heart. It is in the mind, but it goes deeper to a heart issue. When the heart becomes hardened, it restricts our ability to hear and feel. This is why you can bring convincing arguments, but the heart of a person restricts what they can hear and what they are willing to receive. Paul addresses this in his letter to the Corinthians.

> *For though we walk in the flesh, we do not war according to the flesh. For the weapons of our warfare are not carnal but mighty in God for pulling down strongholds, casting down arguments and every high thing that exalts itself against the knowledge of God, bringing every thought into captivity to the obedience of Christ, and being ready to punish all disobedience when your obedience is fulfilled.*

> 2 Corinthians 10:3-5

The life of God is lived out through our flesh. But our weapons in the warfare are not of the flesh nor are they carnal. Casting down the futile thoughts or arguments against God comes through the Word of God declared which deals with high-mindedness and presents obedience to Christ. This can only take place through the authority He has given to us by the power of the Holy Spirit, bringing conviction to the unbeliever. Paul ends his thought by saying every disobedience to God's Word of repentance and salvation brings punishment through our obedience to proclaim.

Notice verse 19 says that there are those that are past feeling because they have chosen to give themselves to lewdness. This is being very sexual or lustful in an offensive way. We live in such a day! Uncleanness, expressing dirtiness, impurity, infected with a supernatural contagion, communication of disease from one person to another by close contact. Does this sound familiar? They are lacking in clarity, precision, conception and execution. They do not have clarity so they cannot execute a proper lifestyle. Not only are they lewd and unclean, but they are also filled with greediness, thinking only of their own lustful desires. Paul seems to be describing much of our culture today.

Let's get out of the mire and into Christ. Verses 20-24 bring contrast with the world.

> *But you have not so learnèd Christ, if indeed you have heard Him and have been taught by Him, as the truth is in Jesus: that you put off, concerning your former conduct, the old man which grows corrupt according to the deceitful lusts, and be renewed in the spirit of your mind, and that you put on the new man which was created according to God, in true righteousness and holiness.*

Ephesians 4:20-24

The above five verses bring a strong contrast with the world. We are on a learning curve of a deeper understanding of our Savior and Lord. We are on a journey of growing in our understanding of the truth. We are developing a discipline of putting off the old man with its corruptness and its deceitful lusts and putting on the new man daily. This is not natural, but a work of the Spirit of God that renews the spirit of our mind.

The new man was created according to God's purpose and not man's purpose. The two key components are righteousness and holiness by the work of the Holy Spirit who is the Spirit of the Father and the Spirit of Christ. Paul begins to outline our responsibility in verse 25. He addresses the Holy Spirit and Paul's exhortation not to grieve God's Spirit who dwells in each believer.

What Have We Learned?

1. Verses 17-24 are a close look at the new man created in Christ Jesus.

2. Our walk is to be totally different than it was when we were unsaved and walking as other Gentiles walk—in the futility of their minds.

3. This was not a makeover but a whole new man or nature given to us through the Holy Spirit.

4. The old man is futile in his pursuits; he has a darkened understanding and is alienated from the life of God. He has ignorance because of the blindness of the heart.

5. This is not how we have learned Christ. We grow in Christ, learning to put off the old man and become renewed in the spirit of our mind.

Ephesians 4:25-32

Therefore, putting away lying, "Let each one of you speak truth with his neighbor," for we are members of one another. "Be angry, and do not sin": do not let the sun go down on your wrath, nor give place to the devil. Let him who stole steal no longer, but rather let him labor, working with his hands what is good, that he may have something to give him who has need. Let no corrupt word proceed out of your mouth, but what is good for necessary edification, that it may impart grace to the hearers. And do not grieve the Holy Spirit of God, by whom you were sealed for the day of redemption. Let all bitterness, wrath, anger, clamor, and evil speaking be put away from you, with all malice. And be kind to one another, tenderhearted, forgiving one another, even as God in Christ forgave you.

Do Not Grieve the Spirit

The first thing Paul deals with is lying, which is replaced with truth through the conversion process brought about by the word of God and the transforming work of the Holy Spirit. In the body of Christ, we are to see each other as our neighbor. In that relationship, we are to speak with one another in truth and in love!

What a contrast to the world! Lying takes on many forms. One might speak an untruth, but one can also live an untruth. Our politics, our media and even sworn testimony today are filled with untruths. It was not always that way. One major shift in our culture over the last 60 years has been the rejection of truth rooted in the eternal, beginning in our educational system. Let me say this, "Truth is eternal and it is absolute. You can trust it; you can build your life on it." Jesus said, "I am the way, the truth, and the life" (John 14:6). Jesus was the personification of truth! How do I know that Adam and Eve were real people? Because Jesus refers to the Garden. How do I know that Abraham lived and was the person Genesis speaks about? Because Jesus established Abraham's centrality. How do I know of Moses' importance? Because Jesus established Moses' importance.

Why is this of top importance? Because Paul makes clear that by the Word of God and the power of the Holy Spirit, every believer is joined as members one of another. If I lie, I am lying to my head, Jesus. If I lie, I am also lying to the body of which I am joined. This is the basis for James' exhortation in James 5:16, "Confess your faults or trespasses to one another, and pray for one another, that you may be healed."

Next, in Ephesians 4:26-27, Paul addresses anger. "Be angry, and do not sin": do not let the sun go down on your wrath, nor give place to the devil." This is one of the most liberating scriptures that you will read. Anger is not just a human emotion; it is divine. God reveals His wrath throughout the scriptures. Jesus became angry. At one point, Jesus addressed His own disciples saying:

> *Then Jesus answered and said, "O faithless and*
> *perverse generation, how long shall I be with you?*
> *How long shall I bear with you? Bring him here to Me.*

> Matthew 17:17

There are times when anger is appropriate. Yet there is never a time to hold on to that anger. Throughout the Bible, we find two things in parallel: 1) salvation and forgiveness, 2) anger and judgment. The true message of the gospel contains both. Repent and receive mercy and grace or continue resisting God's mercy with its salvation, and know His anger and justice instead.

> *Now therefore, be wise, O kings;*
> *Be instructed, you judges of the earth.*
> *Serve the Lord with fear,*
> *And rejoice with trembling.*

> *Kiss the Son, lest He be angry,*
> *And you perish in the way,*
> *When His wrath is kindled but a little.*
> *Blessed are all those who put their trust in Him.*

Psalm 2:10-12

In the life of the believer, holding onto anger is sin and gives place for the enemy in one's life. Jesus made forgiveness a law of the kingdom of God in His teaching of the unforgiving servant in Matthew 18. Unforgiveness gives legal right for the devil's tormentors to torment those in his prison.

Paul continues to instruct the believers in God's New Testament plan for His people.

Verse 28: No more stealing, but give oneself to labor, working with your hands earning an income. Paul calls it good because we not only have money so our needs are met, but we also have money to help others in their need.

Verse 29: Paul deals with corrupt communication coming from a believer's mouth. He commands, "Let no corrupt word come out of your mouth." This covers a lot of territories. Paul instructs us to "Speak what is good for edification." We are members of one another and members of His body. Our goal is to build up and not tear down people. We are called to "Impart grace to the hearers," not negatives, not put-downs, but uplift and edifying others.

Verse 30: Paul puts all of this into the context of not grieving the Holy Spirit. This is the same Holy Spirit who dwells in each believer. Our redemption was sealed by Him. "Sealed for the day of redemption." Everything we do and say should come by the Holy Spirit, affecting our thinking, our conversation, and our lifestyle.

Finally, Paul closes this chapter with two contrasting natures revealed in verses 31-32.

Verse 31: "Let all bitterness, wrath, anger, clamor, and evil speaking be put away from you, with all malice."

In other words, the old man!

Paul names six critical areas that must be removed from our hearts and communications. When Paul says, "Put away from you…" he is not just speaking personally but corporately as well. In other words, Paul is calling us to a culture of honor. I could write a chapter about honor, but verse 32 gives to us a good summary of honor.

Verse 32: "And be kind to one another, tenderhearted, forgiving one another, even as God in Christ forgave you."

What Did We Learn as We Ended Ephesians 4:25-32?

1. First, that lying has no place in the believer's life. We are people of truth. This is a major point because we are members one of another.

2. We learned how to handle anger as a believer—permitted but don't let the sun go down on that anger. Forgive.

3. Holding onto anger is sin and gives a place for the devil.

4. No place for stealing, but instead hard work in the life of the believer.

5. Put away all corrupt communication.

6. Don't grieve the Holy Spirit who is in each believer.

Chapter 5

Ephesians 5:1-7

Therefore be imitators of God as dear children. And walk in love, as Christ also has loved us and given Himself for us, an offering and a sacrifice to God for a sweet-smelling aroma. But fornication and all uncleanness or covetousness, let it not even be named among you, as is fitting for saints; neither filthiness, nor foolish talking, nor coarse jesting, which are not fitting, but rather giving of thanks. For this you know, that no fornicator, unclean person, nor covetous man, who is an idolater, has any inheritance in the kingdom of Christ and God. Let no one deceive you with empty words, for because of these things the wrath of God comes upon the sons of disobedience. Therefore do not be partakers with them.

Walk In Love as Imitators of God

Chapter 5 opens with "Therefore..." The *therefore* is why we review the previous instructions.

Verse 1 tells us to, "Be imitators of God as dear children." This corresponds to John's words: "He who has seen me has seen the Father" (John 14:9). The Spirit of the Father and the Spirit of the Son dwell in the believer. In the believer is His very nature. That is the nature we are to draw from. That nature gives us the ability to be like our Father.

One of the most important things to a parent is that our children reflect our values in their interactions with others. We want them to be courteous, polite, and bring honor to our good family name. Our heavenly Father is expecting no less. His nature is residing in us through the Holy Spirit. Beyond that, the Holy Spirit is there to give to us the mind of Christ. He is there to empower us as children of God. It would be impossible for us to be imitators of God without the Holy Spirit being present as our Helper in all things.

In 2011, the Lord led me to write the devotional book, *A Daily Devotional Developing Your Relationship with the Holy Spirit.* It is a comprehensive devotional bringing together the Word of God and our relationship with the Holy Spirit. It is available for ordering at the City Church Web Site: www.sdccm.org.

I mention the book because the Holy Spirit is the most misunderstood of the Godhead. He is the Spirit of the Father and the Spirit of the Son who came to dwell in each believer. He is the "Helper" promised by Jesus. Promised by Jesus because the Father had promised the Son that their Holy Spirit would be given to all those who trusted Christ (see John chapters 14-16).

In Ephesians 5:1-7, the theme is "walk in love." As John told us: "God is love" (1 John 4:8). Let's read this in context.

> *Beloved, let us love one another, for love is of God; and everyone who loves is born of God and knows God. He who does not love does not know God, for God is love. In this the love of God was manifested toward us, that God has sent His only begotten Son into the world, that we might live through Him. In this is love, not that we loved God, but that He loved us and sent His Son to be the propitiation for our sins. Beloved, if God so loved us, we also ought to love one another.*

1 John 4:7-11

As Christ loved us, He gave Himself for us, an offering, a sacrifice, a sweet-smelling aroma! So here is our measuring stick. Don't you know that we cannot live up to this standard without the power and the life of the Holy Spirit supplying us daily and maybe, many times throughout the day!

The love of God is a love unheard of in the world before Jesus appeared through His birth and gave Himself for mankind on the cross. What a contrast the Apostle Paul draws for us as he represents what the world thinks of love. In verse 3, Paul begins with fornication, uncleanness and covetousness. Fornication is all sexual impurity outside of marriage, but also includes adultery between married couples. We live in a time that uncleanness is no longer hidden. With the pornography industry doing billions of dollars a year in sales, with the looseness of values in the cable television industry, and with sexual values being lowered throughout the culture, and with the sanctity of marriage under full attack we have become an unclean society that has given demonic forces full access to the lives of multitudes.

All this leads to covetousness. That is, wanting what is not your right to have or what is not legal for you to possess.

Covetous; adjective

1. marked by inordinate desire for wealth or possessions or for another's possessions

2. having a craving for possession, to include covetous of power

Paul puts this word in the context of sexual impurity: desiring sexual involvement with others that belong to another and desiring power over another's body.

In this third verse, Paul adds, "Let it not even be named among you, as is fitting for saints." We need to get back to the apostolic view of being saintly. A saint, in the biblical sense, is a sanctified individual. In other words, one set apart for the Lord and His pleasure; one who is holy because He is Holy.

Verse 4 continues with a list of worldly activities, "Neither filthiness, nor foolish talking, nor coarse jesting, which are not fitting, but rather giving of thanks." The saint of God is known by their attitude

ortrt

of gratitude, not only for God's love to them but also for the saints of God and the high calling of God in Christ Jesus our Lord.

Let's read what Paul has to say to the Philippian saints.

> *Not that I have already attained, or am already perfected; but I press on, that I may lay hold of that for which Christ Jesus has also laid hold of me. Brethren, I do not count myself to have apprehended; but one thing I do, forgetting those things which are behind and reaching forward to those things which are ahead, I press toward the goal for the prize of the upward call of God in Christ Jesus.*
>
> *Therefore let us, as many as are mature, have this mind; and if in anything you think otherwise, God will reveal even this to you. Nevertheless, to the degree that we have already attained, let us walk by the same rule, let us be of the same mind.*

Philippians 3:12-16

In verse 5, Paul speaks of inheritance. "Fornicators, unclean persons, nor a covetous man, who is an idolater, has any inheritance in the kingdom of Christ and God."

Fornication, uncleanness, and covetousness are all part of idolatry as seen throughout the Old Testament. These three areas are connected to a false worship. The Old Testament called it Baal worship. Baal was an idol with demonic entities empowering the three areas of fornication, uncleanness, and covetousness, which were central to the idolatry worship of the Baals led by false prophets. All this is highlighted in 1 Kings chapters 16-19 in King Ahab and Jezebel's life. It was Elijah the Prophet who confronted the King and Queen. He exposed them for what they were and foretold their end...and it was not pretty.

The kingdom of God is so separated from the kingdom of darkness, there is no place for compromise. Only the blood of Jesus and His righteous sacrifice is powerful enough to break these strongholds of sexual bondage fueled by demonic powers. The filling of the Holy Spirit, "Endued with power from on high," is what will defeat the Baals of sexual perversion and uncleanness with covetousness in the life of the saints of God. Rise up oh man of God, rise up oh women of God in today's culture, and declare the kingdom of God through the Holy Spirit's power. It is the mandate of the Lord's church to establish righteousness on the earth by discipling the nations to Christ and His purity and cleanness in holiness.

Verses 6 and 7 sum up Paul's heart and passion for Christ.

> *Let no one deceive you with empty words, for because of these things the wrath of God comes upon the sons of disobedience. Therefore do not be partakers with them.*

There are many empty words out there. There are many empty lives today that are trying to get satisfaction through empty efforts of the flesh, sexual impurities and all kinds of covetousness in idolatry. God has an inheritance in His kingdom that satisfies and fulfills everything one could desire with eternal satisfaction.

What Have We Learned?

1. We are to be imitators of God as dear children.

2. We are to walk in love, for God is love.

3. Put away fornication, uncleanness, and covetousness.

4. We are saints, meaning He has sanctified the believer and set him apart for righteousness.

5. Our inheritance comes from the cleansing of Christ. Those who practice fornication, uncleanness, and covetousness have no inheritance in God's kingdom.

6. Deception comes through empty words, and it brings the wrath of God.

7. Believers are not to be partakers with those who practice such things.

Ephesians 5:8-13

For you were once darkness, but now you are light in the Lord. Walk as children of light (for the fruit of the Spirit is in all goodness, righteousness, and truth), finding out what is acceptable to the Lord. And have no fellowship with the unfruitful works of darkness, but rather expose them. For it is shameful even to speak of those things which are done by them in secret. But all things that are exposed are made manifest by the light, for whatever makes manifest is light.

Once Darkness but Now You Are Light

As we continue in Ephesians chapter 5, we are picking up with verse 8: "For you were once darkness, but now you are light in the Lord. Walk as children of light." Paul cannot be any clearer than he is here.

Remember the warning of verse 7: "Therefore do not be partakers with them."

Paul had listed works of darkness that, as Gentiles, these saints once were part of, but now they have been translated out of those works of darkness and into God's marvelous light (see Colossians 1:13).

Paul is speaking of our daily life in Christ. "Walk as children of the light." It is not about Sunday-go-to-church people." This is speaking to the new man. This is speaking to 24-hour saints of God. This addresses our witness as light in the world. You see, God chose to create His Son's body in the world among darkness, not in heaven among angels!

The first creation was perfect until the serpent tempted Eve, and she in turn tempted Adam, who brought down man in what is called the "fall." Sin began to reign through God's creation man. In Christ, salvation has come, and a new creation of the Spirit was begun, here on planet earth. It is growing as fallen man is convicted of sin and Satan's dominion in the nation's fads. As fallen man is convicted of righteousness that is imputed through Christ and lived out through those translated from the kingdom of darkness into the kingdom of God's dear Son. As conviction of judgment comes to man's heart and he realizes that Christ bore the judgment on his behalf. That if one does not receive God's provision in Christ, an eternal judgment lies ahead where there is no escape.

Verse 9 reveals what kind of light should be shinning from the life of the children of God. "For the fruit of the Spirit is in all goodness, righteousness, and truth." If the goodness of God rules in us, if the righteousness of God is established in us, and if truth is our practice, then all of the other manifestations of the Spirit named in Galatians 5 will also be visible and be light in us as we light a darkened world.

Verse 10 gives to us our assignment: "Finding out what is acceptable to the Lord." This verse helps define our daily relationship with Christ Jesus. Studying the scriptures is our most important resource in coming to know the Lord's will in all things. Developing our relationship with the Holy Spirit is also necessary. The Lord did not leave us to figure it all out on our own. We have been made alive in the Spirit so that our life is now intended to be lived by the Spirit, not fulfilling the lusts of the flesh. For that matter, we are not to trust in the flesh.

Trust in the Lord with all your heart,
And lean not on your own understanding;
In all your ways acknowledge Him,
And He shall direct your paths.
Do not be wise in your own eyes;
Fear the Lord and depart from evil.
It will be health to your flesh,
And strength to your bones.

Proverbs 3:5-8

Verse 11 raises questions for us. How do we live in this darkened world if we are not to have fellowship with the unfruitful works of darkness? What did Paul mean by fellowship? He certainly did not mean we are not to have contact with people who are in darkness. The word fellowship is connected with the word devotion in Acts 2:42. We are not to desire or enter into any kind of participation with darkness and the evil deeds of darkness. We are not to be devoted to the practice of darkness and the evil connected to the darkness. We are called to light. The darkness means there are times when we must shine in the darkness.

An example for me came in the early 70s. Working for a television repair company, I associated with a number of people who were far from the Lord in their social practices. During the year they would get together on a social level. There was drinking, dancing with one another's wives, not-so-nice storytelling, and the cursing issue (with Our Father's name being abused often). Well, I had no need for the activity so I did not attend. Some took offense, like I was better than they were. They did not understand my values. And quite frankly, I did not like theirs.

One Christmas the Lord spoke to me to go to the company Christmas party. I really did not want to go. The Lord explained to me that it was okay and taught me how to respond. He said to be there in the beginning as people just began to arrive. He said to stay until they became drunk. And when they began to swap partners in dancing, just politely excuse yourself. "They will remember that you were there and appreciate your coming, but will not miss you when the drinking begins." It was true, and it opened doors of communication that I had not previously had.

We are in the world, but not of the world. We are not to be snobs, but we are to seek the Lord for wisdom on how to relate to the unregenerate that they might be won through our good deeds. One way of exposing the "unfruitful works of darkness" is by simply being the light in the way we conduct our lifestyle and live out our values. People will notice our lifestyle without our pointing it out. There are times when we must speak and expose the works of darkness.

There have been times when I could not hold my peace but had to address clear sin and works of darkness even if it meant losing my job. One person wanted me to answer his questions, but instead of allowing me to speak, he communicated his views. I told him that the difference between him and myself was that his highest authority was between his ears. In other words, he was full of pride. I told him my authority comes from a book, the Bible. There have been many times I've called people out on their sins, attitudes, disrespect, and views that were clearly ungodly.

Verse 12 speaks to shameful sexual things done in secret by those who are associated with darkness. Paul tells us that it "is shameful even to speak of those things which are done by them in secret."

In verse 13, Paul points out that "all things that are exposed are made manifest by the light, for whatever makes manifest is light." Light exposes the darkness. As believers walk together in the light, the light becomes stronger or brighter in exposing the darkness. As one examines oneself, the question should be, am I shining as light in accordance to God's grace of fruit in my life? As we make manifest the darkness, it becomes clearer and clearer that we are light! We are living in a day of light. In other words, light is in the world through the saints of God, making manifest the darkness.

This takes us back to verse 9: "The fruit of the Spirit is in all goodness, righteousness, and truth."

- Goodness: Jesus said, "There is none good, but God" The goodness is God's goodness dwelling in us. Not our goodness measured on a human level, but His goodness which can only manifest through His life which dwells in the true believer who has surrendered their life to Christ in baptism in death, burial, and resurrection life initiated by the Spirit of God in the believer's regeneration.

- Righteousness: righteousness is the result of Christ's finished work in the cross. He is the righteous one and His righteousness is imputed to the believer. I am righteous because He is the Righteous One.

- Truth: Jesus Christ is truth personified! "I am the way, the truth, and the life. No man comes to the Father except through Me." What Jesus is saying to His disciples, is not an abstract statement. Unfortunately, that is how many hear and apply His statement. He says this in the context of the promised coming of the Holy Spirit after His enthronement.

I will pray the Father, and He will give you another Helper, that He may abide with you forever—the Spirit of truth, whom the world cannot receive, because it neither sees Him nor knows Him; but you know Him, for He dwells with you and will be in you

John 14:16-17

When Jesus came in the flesh, He was seen by the world, but the world did not know Him. Even His own covenant people rejected Him. But to those who received Him, to them gave He power to become the children of God (see John 1:12). Remember Ephesians 5:1: "Imitators of God as dear children."

Here is the proof of our identity as dear children of God: Christ is in us by the indwelling Holy Spirit. We are to be light through goodness, righteousness, and truth. Our testimony is to the world and to the darkness in the world. We are liberators as the children of light!

What Have We Learned?

1. We are now light and delivered from the darkness.

2. We are children of light so walk in the light.

3. God is creating His Son's body in the world among darkness and not in heaven among angels.

4. Our light is manifested in the fruit of the Spirit.

5. Our assignment is to discover what is pleasing to God our Father in heaven.

6. We are to live in the darkness and be His light.

7. The light of God is meant to be manifested as a corporate body, not as independent and individual lights.

8. In us is the nature of the one who is the light of the world, Christ Jesus Our Lord.

Ephesians 5:14-21

Therefore He says:

> *"Awake, you who sleep,*
> *Arise from the dead,*
> *And Christ will give you light."*

See then that you walk circumspectly, not as fools but as wise, redeeming the time, because the days are evil.

Therefore do not be unwise, but understand what the will of the Lord is. And do not be drunk with wine, in which is dissipation; but be filled with the Spirit, speaking to one another in psalms and hymns and spiritual songs, singing and making melody in your heart to the Lord, giving thanks always for all things to God the Father in the name of our Lord Jesus Christ, submitting to one another in the fear of God.

Walk This Way

Paul supports the views he shared about our being "light in a dark world" with verses from Isaiah 26:19 and 61:1. These are Messianic verses that highlight Christ who is God's light to humanity. Jesus is the light-bearer and the light-imparter. It is Christ who gives us light!

For this reason, Paul instructs us to "walk circumspectly," in verse 15. Circumspectly definition: "Careful to consider all circumstances and possible consequences: *prudent* i.e., diplomacy required a circumspect response; or they are circumspect in all their business dealings." (Merriam-Webster Dictionary).

Paul uses strong language in making his point: "walk circumspectly, not as fools." I am sorry to say that in my many years of ministry, I have seen many people who claim to be Christian, yet they walk as fools and not wise as Paul admonishes us here. The range of foolishness is from personal character, marriage relationship, parenting, financial responsibility, and so much more. Part of being children of light encompasses wisdom. Consider what Solomon counsels:

> *To know wisdom and instruction,*
> *To perceive the words of understanding,*
> *To receive the instruction of wisdom*
> *Justice, judgment, and equity.*

Proverbs 1:2-3

> *The fear of the Lord is the beginning of knowledge,*
> *But fools despise wisdom and instruction.*

Proverbs 1:7

Paul, in verse 16, helps us to understand that part of wisdom is redeeming the time. How careful are we concerning the time we have been allotted? Do we waste our time on nothingness or wisely think about our time investment? I say investment, because how we spend our time will determine how productive we become.

On a personal note, I will mention my time investment many years ago in the study of the word of God. As a young man, I would always take notes of sermons and teachings I was sitting under. I would study those notes by personally looking up passages of scripture, doing word studies and meditating on what was taught. I also would share with others what I was learning. I did not realize it at the time, but God used that investment of my time to produce a solid biblical understanding which enabled me to discern error from the truth and provide a healthy knowledge of God's Word for my future preparation in the Ephesian 4:11 gifts given by Jesus to His body. A quote from Charles Studd (1860 to 1931) that I heard many years ago has greater meaning to me in my later years:

> *Only one life 'twill soon be past.*
> *Only what's done for Christ will last.*

142

Paul goes on to say: "Redeeming the time, because the days are evil." It is easy to find ourselves absorbed by the culture of the day, that is, accepting cultural norms rather than biblical values. I am not sure how many Christians are caught up in this, but I know that it is many. Maybe the root of the problem is that many believers never really got free from the world and its thinking. One of the greatest issues within the church community today is the issue of mixture, that is, mixing the world's system with church community life. The Bible does not deal with this subject in the context of the church, at least in the way we understand church today. The Bible deals with this subject of a mixture by contrasting the kingdom of darkness with the kingdom of light. It is important for believers today to get back to the biblical understanding of the battles we face in the light of biblical teaching on light and darkness as the chief issue. I am sure this is a mouth full and for some; it may be hard to understand and or receive.

In verse 17 Paul states: "Therefore do not be unwise, but understand what the will of the Lord is." Help me, Jesus! As His dear children, we have as a priority to learn the will of our Lord. When we keep the fruit of the Spirit in mind, we will know the will of the Lord. Note Paul's contrast of "drunk" and be "filled with the Spirit." When drunk with wine, it leads to dissipation and dissipated living. It can be a descent into drunkenness and sexual dissipation. Also, it can lead to the squandering of money, energy, or resources.

In verse 18, Paul looks back on how the world thinks and acts, when he says, "And do not be drunk with wine, in which is dissipation."

Dissipation - noun:

1. dissipated living. "a descent into drunkenness and sexual dissipation"

2. the squandering of money, energy, or resources.

Similar to: debauchery, decadence, dissoluteness immoderation immorality, sinfulness

Google's English dictionary

Paul's admonition in verse 18 is to be "filled with the Spirit." Even though we received the Holy Spirit when we were born of the Spirit, we leak easily. Our need is to be continually filled with the Holy Spirit.

In verse 19, Paul tells us how this is done. "Speaking to one another in psalms and hymns and spiritual songs, singing and making melody in your heart to the Lord." Worship is the key to helping us have a Spirit-filled life.

Verse 20: Along with worship is learning to give thanks always. "Giving thanks always for all things to God the Father in the name of our Lord Jesus Christ."

Then in verse 21, Paul speaks of submitting to one another in the fear of God (see Philippians 2:3-9). Submitting to one another in the fear of God is found in living out the lifestyle of the Spirit-filled believer in worship, encouragement, creating melody in your heart before God, and always giving Him thanks for all things in the authority of our Lord Jesus Christ. Paul speaks of this as "submitting to one another in the fear of God."

These areas do not just happen. It requires commitment on our part, that is, a disciplined lifestyle, purposely cutting off those things that distract us from the Lord's presence and His joy. We must purposely focus our attention on the kingdom of God and His righteousness.

"In the fear of God" (v 21) is an outstanding place to begin our discussion of family relationship. Let me begin by defining the fear of God. Paul is not saying to God's people: do this because we are afraid of God. No, it is because we reverence God who is our Father in heaven. When we think of the word *submission*, it should be thought of in terms of reverence and respect for our heavenly Father. Another way of looking at this admonition is through the word *honor*. It is a culture of honor that the Lord desires to develop in our hearts and in our lifestyle. It begins in the family and then extends to the community of believers.

Let's Review What We Have Learned

1. We are to walk in wisdom, which meant circumspectly, not as fools but as wise.

2. As His people, we are not to be drunk on wine or alcohol, but we are to be filled with the Spirit.

3. Our daily mode should be one of worship and thanksgiving.

4. As believers in Christ, we are to submit ourselves one to another in the fear of God and with thanksgiving in all things to God the Father in the name of our Lord Jesus Christ.

Ephesians 5:22-33

Wives, submit to your own husbands, as to the Lord. For the husband is head of the wife, as also Christ is head of the church; and He is the Savior of the body. Therefore, just as the church is subject to Christ, so let the wives be to their own husbands in everything.

Husbands, love your wives, just as Christ also loved the church and gave Himself for her, that He might sanctify and cleanse her with the washing of water by the word, that He might present her to Himself a glorious church, not having spot or wrinkle or any such thing, but that she should be holy and without blemish. So husbands ought to love their own wives as their own bodies; he who loves his wife loves himself. For no one ever hated his own flesh, but nourishes and cherishes it, just as the Lord does the church. For we are members of His body, of His flesh and of His bones. "For this reason a man shall leave his father and mother and be joined to his wife, and the two shall become one flesh." This is a great mystery, but I speak concerning Christ and the church. Nevertheless let each one of you in particular so love his own wife as himself, and let the wife see that she respects her husband.

Family Life from A Kingdom Covenant Perspective

In verse 22, Paul begins to teach the saints about family life which is the core of sharing testimony and life in community. Consider how family life, including the marriage relationship, is the great testimony to the world in portraying the intimate relationship with our Lord that Paul calls "a great mystery," speaking concerning Christ and the church.

Ephesians 5:22-6:4 deals with the new creation family, not trying to fix Adam's family but creating a redeemed family by the Spirit through our Lord Jesus Christ who ever lives to make intercession for His new creation men and women and their children. We begin to look at Ephesians 5:22-33, which is speaking about family relationship as it relates to the Lord Jesus and His church. Paul begins with the wife's role in the marriage relationship.

Family Relationship and Christ and His Church

In this next segment, Paul gives us clear teaching regarding the family relationship in the New Testament under the Lordship of Jesus Christ. As we have seen in previous chapters, the New Testament stands in the foundation of a new creation of the Spirit through the love of God manifested in the blood of Jesus Christ and His broken body. The result is a new man who is the creation of the Holy Spirit revealed as the last Adam, raised from the dead. Jesus is the last Adam (see 1 Corinthians 15:45). He is the end of Adam's race and the beginning of His Race. A new family is beginning on the earth. It is the family of God! It is men and women born of the Spirit and married in the Lord— a family meant to raise children that are dedicated to the Lord and His kingdom purposes in extending the Kingdom of God in the generations to come.

This is the foundation with which we must understand Paul's teaching regarding the wife and the husband and the children of a godly home. With that in mind, look at verse 22: "Wives, submit to your own husbands, as to the Lord."

For the Christian wife, it is larger than just submitting to a human being who is your husband. Paul says that it is a matter of your submission to the Lord. Let me be very clear. What Paul is addressing is in the context of Christian values. I do not believe Paul is speaking of cruelty, spousal abuse, and clear sinful activities that the Bible classifies as partakers of those living in darkness.

Paul's instruction to wives is in the context of headship and accountability. In Matthew 19:4-6, Jesus answers the Pharisees who were trying to trick Jesus with a question about divorce. Jesus establishes God's order of marriage by reciting Genesis 1:27 and 5:2 He created them male and female, and He blessed them. Here we see the beginning of mankind: male and female. First the male, then out of the male He created the female. God is a god of first mention. In other words, the first mention sets the order going forward. This order was set prior to the fall or sin of man when mankind first disrespected their creator by submitting to the enemy of God and the enemy of God's creation made in His image. The man, Adam, was created first, then the woman. Adam first received God's Word and he instructed the women. We see this in Genesis by implication, but Paul confirms it in 1 Corinthians 11 as he addresses the purpose and order of the creation of mankind.

These are very difficult scriptures when we try to interpret and understand them in our culture. Do not get bogged down with minors when the major point Paul is making has to do with godly order in the home for the sake of the Kingdom of God. In other words, an ordered family life that gives testimony of God's kingdom at work on the earth and at the same time resists the enemy and his attacks.

I hope this gives clarity and understanding to what Paul is saying to the Lord's daughters in their relationship with their husbands who are sons of God.

Verse 23 adds: "For the husband is head of the wife, as Christ is head of the church; and He is the Savior of the body." It should be clear that headship is very important in understanding the functioning of God's kingdom "on earth as it is in heaven." In Jesus' ministry, headship is prominent. In Matthew 8, the centurion saw that Jesus' authority came from His submission to authority over Him. The centurion knew all Jesus had to do was speak the word, and his servant would be healed. He understood that Jesus' power came from His Head which was His heavenly Father. Headship and authority are closely related. Proper relationship regarding headship releases authority in a respective area such as family. Headship is not forced but instead comes through humility. Philippians 2 describes our Lord's humility which brought Him to the place of receiving from His Father all authority in heaven and on earth.

In love, the Father gives headship to the man with the expectation that headship would operate in and through love. In the man's headship, he always has the wife and her welfare in mind. In love, the wife receives her husband's headship, recognizing he did not take it but received it from Christ. So, she is really submitting to the Lord.

Verse 24: "Therefore, just as the church is subject to Christ, so let the wives be to their own husbands in everything." It does not get any clearer for the wife than what this verse states as to the connection of submission to her husband. The church is the bride of Christ but is also His body. Note the words: "In everything." I mentioned early that these are not easy to understand or receive scriptures. It takes commitment to Christ and the grace of the Holy Spirit. It will require specific prayer by asking the Holy Spirit for His help in grace and in faith to be the kingdom wife that Paul is describing.

Can you see in verses 23-24 how close all this is related to Christ and His Church? It really is a kingdom matter; it is a supernatural matter, not a natural work like in Adam but supernatural in Christ through the Holy Spirit. As Christ is the Savior of the body, so the husband is to be the savior, protector and strength for his wife.

Verse 25 now moves the full attention to the husband.

Husbands, love your wives, just as Christ also loved the church and gave Himself for her.

This can only come through headship. The head of every man is Christ. Husbands cannot do this in their ability. Remember, we are speaking of a new-creation husband. A man who is led by the Spirit of God should be consistent in loving his wife.

The standard of love that Paul gives is how the man loves his own body. Men, we all are careful to nourish our own bodies, and sometimes we overdo it regarding our love for food. We cherish our bodies in many different ways. You can evaluate this in regard to your own life. We spend a lot of time thinking about ourselves. How does that compare to how much time we give to thinking about our wife?

Again, Paul reminds us of the Lord and His body—His church. Remember what the scripture says: "Bone of my bones, and flesh of my flesh" (Genesis 2:23). It is hard because we tend to see our wife as a separate entity, but God sees a married couple as one, united by the word of God. This is one example of "Put on the mind of Christ." The one who loves his wife loves himself. Every man needs to re-evaluate his love for his wife. Saying to her, "I love you" is good, but demonstrating that love through careful evaluation is even better. Love needs attention, service, maintenance, and adjustments. Knowing your wife's love language is a good starting place. Keeping short accounts is another helpful practice such as asking for forgiveness and making what your wife shares with you a high priority.

In verse 26, Paul writes concerning Christ and His church; so a man is to give himself for his wife. As Jesus washes His church with the cleansing water of the word, a man should wash his wife with God's word ruling in his life so that his conversation toward his wife is a washing, a cleansing, and an edifying that builds her up consistently. Again, this is not something that naturally comes from the natural man but is a work of the Holy Spirit leadership.

Verse 27 puts the focus fully back on Jesus who desires to present the church "to Himself a glorious church, not having spot or wrinkle or any such thing, but that she should be holy and without blemish."

In the same manner, Paul goes on to say: "Husbands ought to love their wives as their own bodies. He who loves his wife loves himself" (v 28).

150

Then in verse 29, Paul explains, "For no one ever hated his own flesh, but nourishes and cherishes it, just as the Lord does the church." So husbands, let's put "nourish and cherish" into our vocabulary and our thinking regarding our wives. In other words, making the building of her up as a major priority and cherishing her a major focus of our communication toward her.

Verse 30: In the covenant relationship we have with Christ, we are members of His body, of His flesh, and of His bones. The same is true within the marriage covenant as a man and a woman leave their natural parental family and are joined to one another, becoming "one flesh."

> *"For this reason a man shall leave his father and mother and be joined to his wife, and the two shall become one flesh." This is a great mystery, but I speak concerning Christ and the church.*

Ephesians 5:31-32

Verse 32 speaks of this as a great mystery as it is with Christ and His church. So, the end of Paul's instruction to husbands and wives is cast in love and respect. This is what a culture of honor truly looks like.

The word *leave* in this verse is pretty important. We all received certain core values when growing up. Some values are good, while others are troublesome. Every young couple planning to be married should make a list of the values with which they were raised. Then decide which are good and which are not so good. Then together agree on their core values that will help define their marriage and agreed upon core commitments.

Paul says, "This is a great mystery." The understanding of becoming one is a mystery, but Paul is speaking of that mystery he began with, the one new man, and how we are made one with Christ as a member of His body joined with others.

Paul's summary and our conclusion are found in verse 33.

Nevertheless let each one of you in particular so love his own wife as himself, and let the wife see that she respects her husband.

This verse makes it clear that Paul is getting personal, yes, speaking to the body of believers, but also to each one in particular. This is personal for each one of us. I am commanded to love my wife as myself. My wife is instructed to respect me. Christ's love for His church was demonstrated in giving His life for her.

What We Have Learned

1. Jesus began by setting the first creation with Adam and Eve back into the original order which He and the Father through the Spirit created in the garden.

2. Wives are to be submitted to their husbands in the Lord.

3. The relationship between a husband and wife is a picture of the relationship of Jesus and His Church.

4. The order first given in the garden is the same order between Christ and His church. First Christ, then the church.

5. Godly order in the home gives us a kingdom picture of how we are to relate with Christ.

6. The husband carries the headship of his household and he is seen as the savior of his wife as Christ is the Savior of His body—the church.

7. Husbands ought to love their wives as their own body, even as the Lord loves His church.

8. All of what Paul is teaching in these verses is a great mystery.

   For no one ever hated his own flesh, but nourishes and cherishes it, just as the Lord does *the church. For we are members of His body, of His flesh and of His bones.*

   Ephesians 5:29-30

Chapter 6

Ephesians 6:1-4

Children, obey your parents in the Lord, for this is right. "Honor your father and mother," which is the first commandment with promise: "that it may be well with you and you may live long on the earth." And you, fathers, do not provoke your children to wrath, but bring them up in the training and admonition of the Lord.

Parents and Children

As we begin chapter 6, we hear Paul's instruction to children beginning with verse 1: "Children, obey your parents in the Lord, for this is right." Again, this is *in the Lord*. Parents should be praying for their children while they're in the womb. As children are born, parents are to receive them with thanksgiving and commit them to the Lord and His plans and purposes, nurturing and cherishing children from their very beginning and throughout their development. A healthy, biblical relationship of father and mother in their marriage will go a long way in shaping the children for God's kingdom purpose. A culture of honor is a key for children to honor their fathers and mothers, which is the first commandment with promise (see Exodus 20:12). That promise includes doing well and living a long life. Children learn through observing the honor that transpires between their parents. Of course, the opposite is also true.

A major key for children is Paul's instruction to the fathers in verse 4: "And you, fathers, do not provoke your children to wrath but bring them up in the training and admonition of the Lord."

A major challenge in raising children is the issue of a child with a strong will. Real skill and patience are needed to break the will without breaking the child's spirit and creating lifetime damage. I would like to share three examples as a father in raising three of our seven children.

Some personal testimony

At age 4, my son Paul was set in his will to not eat salad. One evening I was determined to help him with that determination because I knew eating salad was healthy and good for him. I told my wife, Becky, to go ahead of us to a church meeting and that Paul and I would be along soon. "Soon" became two hours as Paul dug in, determined not to eat his salad. I too dug in, determined he would. I never got angry; I received grace to patiently wait it out. Eventually, Paul surrendered his will to mine.

Not only did he learn to eat salad and eventually enjoy it, but he and his will also became easier to work with. Today, Paul is a parent and has learned how to deal with the will of his children in the Lord. He and his children have a wonderful relationship.

At age 12, my son Derek had the assignment of cutting the grass in the backyard. I had agreed to pay him for his work. When he thought he was finished, he came to collect his money. I said, "Let's go see how you did." The grass was cut, but not around the edges. I brought this to his attention. He finished the job and again came to be paid. I paid him the agreed amount, but he believed it should be more because of the edge work. He was quite upset with me. Later in life, he told me the story of how he felt, how angry he was, but he also told me it shaped how he holds his subcontractors to a high level of excellence in their work for him.

My son Joseph, who is our youngest, was 15 and under discipline for some areas we were dealing with in his life. One evening, something came to my attention that needed to be addressed. I had company, so I asked Joseph to step outside in the back. He would not move, so I helped him. He was very angry with me and told me so. I too was angry that he had not willingly obeyed and would not cooperate in answering my questions. The Lord spoke to me by asking me the question: "Who is the adult in the place?" I realized I must temper my temper. He was no longer a child that I should spank, but a young man that needed his will to be broken. But I had to be careful not to break his spirit. Later God showed me that some of his problems were developmental. Today, he and I can talk with great freedom and at times, he asks for my advice and input.

Whatever our age may be, we need to always be praying for the next generation, for their hearts to be open and prepared to be called and used by the Lord for their generation.

Reviewing What We Learned:

1. A culture of honor is key to how children learn to honor their parents.

2. Children honoring and obeying their parents is the first commandment with promise.

3. Parents should be praying for their children from the womb and for the rest of their lives.

4. A Father must not create an atmosphere of provoking their children to anger.

5. Understand the difference between the spirit of the child and the will of a child.

Ephesians 6:5-9

Bondservants, be obedient to those who are your masters according to the flesh, with fear and trembling, in sincerity of heart, as to Christ; not with eye service, as men-pleasers, but as bondservants of Christ, doing the will of God from the heart, with goodwill doing service, as to the Lord, and not to men, knowing that whatever good anyone does, he will receive the same from the Lord, whether he is a slave or free. And you, masters, do the same things to them, giving up threatening, knowing that your own Master also is in heaven, and there is no partiality with Him.

Bondservants and Masters

Now we will take a look at Ephesians 6:5-9, which speaks to the transforming power of the Kingdom of God in bondservants and masters, or in today's language, the relationship of employee and employer.

Let's explore word meanings here.

Bondservant; noun: "a person bound in service without wages, a slave or serf."

A bondservant is a slave. Basically, the only difference is that a bondservant is owned as a slave. An indentured servant is more or less working off a debt. He is under contract until the debt is fulfilled.

As a point of interest relating to the subject of bondservants, our first President, George Washington, who owned slaves, wrote in his last will and testament.

> *Item Upon the decease of my wife, it is my Will and desire, that all the slaves which I hold in my own right, shall receive their freedom. To emancipate them during her life, would, tho' earnestly wished by me, be*

> *attended with such insuperable difficulties on account of their intermixture by Marriage of other slave owners.*

He also willed that all those of old age or bodily infirmities, and infancy who cannot support themselves.

> *It is my Will and desire that all who come under the first and second description shall be comfortably clothed and fed by my heirs while they live.*

Some believe that slavery was part of the DNA of America. I believe that George Washington's Last Will and Testimony gives witness that in the heart of our first President was a biblical understanding that slavery was wrong and abhorrent. An act of his choice stated his will to see this atrocity eventually done away with. The DNA of true freedom was in George Washington because of the gospel of our Lord Jesus Christ.

Under Roman rule, slavery was a reality, and the Gospel of the Kingdom was at work both in the bondservant and in the master who owned his bondservant. A personal opinion is that slavery would have ended a long time before it did if the church had not fallen away from her true mandate of discipling nations, bringing them by the Holy Spirit under the rule of King Jesus who is the liberator and emancipator of all.

So, under the present situation of which Paul is writing, controlled by Rome, Paul instructs the bondservants to "be obedient to those who are your masters according to the flesh, with fear and trembling, in the sincerity of heart, as to Christ." Notice the theme "in Christ." Biblical submission is always in Christ or unto Christ. We have been buried with Him in baptism. Our life belongs to Him. We are not our own any longer. Paul recognized masters according to the flesh. He understood the bondage and the darkness of the world, but he also knew that a whole new world was being created. He understood that even in this flesh condition, God could produce a new heart in man, whether that person was Jew or Gentile, bond or free, male or female.

We need to examine our hearts. This is where the real issues lie concerning class, social issues, and justice issues.

He has shown you, O man, what is good;
And what does the Lord require of you
But to do justly,
To love mercy,
And to walk humbly with your God?

Micah 6:8

How can a young man cleanse his way?
By taking heed according to Your word.
With my whole heart I have sought You;
Oh, let me not wander from Your commandments!
Your word I have hidden in my heart,
That I might not sin against You.

Psalm 119:9-11

So, the sincerity of the heart is the issue, which leads to verse 6: "Not with eyeservice, as man pleasers, but as bondservants of Christ, doing the will of God from the heart." Paul is saying don't be looking for or expecting the man to see what you are doing for good. Do it unto the Lord and know that He is watching your good work. Do everything for the Lord and unto Him. Paul goes on to say, "Doing the will of God from the heart." Again, we see it is about our hearts. It is in the inner man that transformation happens and it is the heart that God is looking on.

What comes from the believer's heart is goodwill. All our service is to be unto the Lord and not to men. What an attitude the Lord wants to give to His people! Paul reminds us "that whatever good anyone does, he will receive the same from the Lord, whether he is a slave or free."

Finally, Paul turns his attention to masters. Verse 9: Paul says, "And you, masters, do the same things to them, giving up threatening, knowing that your own Master also is in heaven, and there is no partiality with Him."

The Lord used these scriptures to teach me lifelong understandings that have served me well. When I went to work in 1967 for a large electronics company, the Lord told me how I was to behave. He said to me, "Make your boss a success and I will make you a success." He also said not to ask for a raise. He assured me that if I served Him, He would make sure I was taken care of. The Lord was faithful. I was honored and taken care of by the Lord through my employer. They never knew of my secret agreement with my Savior and Lord. In the seven years I worked for the company, I never asked for a raise but received one every three months. Years later, my former manager, Don, wanted to hire me to run a business he had bought. That was not the Lord's plan, but I appreciated Don reaching out and asking me. God is good!

We are being equipped daily for the spiritual battles of life. Paul teaches us how to be fitted with God's armor for the battles so we might stand strong in the Lord. Our strength and power come from His might.

Ephesians 6:10

Finally, my brethren, be strong in the Lord and in the power of His might

The Whole Armor of God

Here's what we've covered, bringing us to the armor of God.

Ephesians 1:3	Redemption in Christ
Ephesians 1:15	Prayer for Spiritual Wisdom
Ephesians 2:1	By Grace Through Faith
Ephesians 2:11	Brought Near by His Blood
Ephesians 2:19	Christ our Cornerstone
Ephesians 3:1	The Mystery Revealed
Ephesians 3:8	Purpose of the Mystery
Ephesians 3:14	Appreciation of the Mystery
Ephesians 4:1	Walk in Unity
Ephesians 4:7	Spiritual Gifts
Ephesians 4:17	The New Man
Ephesians 4:25	Do Not Grieve the Spirit
Ephesians 5:1	Walk in Love
Ephesians 5:8	Walk in Light
Ephesians 5:15	Walk in Wisdom
Ephesians 5:22	Marriage: Christ and the Church
Ephesians 6:1	Parents and Children
Ephesians 6:5	Bondservants and Masters

Paul begins with the word *finally*. He uses this frequently in the concluding portion of his epistles, introducing practical exhortations, not necessarily implying that the letter is drawing to a close, but marking a transition in the subject matter. (From Vine's Expository Dictionary of Biblical Words, Copyright © 1985, Thomas Nelson Publishers.)

It is true that the subject of the armor of God is the last main subject that Paul deals with in this epistle. It is also the beginning of a larger understanding of the Lord's purpose which He has accomplished in His one new man coming out of every nation. We must have an understanding of the battle in which we are all engaged. Without the proper armor, we will suffer loss. But with an understanding of each piece of armor, we will be equipped for the battle.

I remember when I was drafted into the military in 1965. The first process was boot camp, where I learned about the clothing and equipment I would be wearing into battle as well as the weapons of warfare I would use. I needed training in the use of and upkeep of those weapons. The more I understood about my equipment, the better prepared I was to engage the enemy with a view of defeating him.

One of the major functions of boot camp was to get the soldiers in shape. We would need to be strong and fit for what we would encounter in the battles ahead. For the believer, our strength is found in the Lord and the power of His might. Believers do not trust in their strength because it is not sufficient for spiritual warfare. After all, we are engaged with a supernatural force that can only be overcome through the strength and power of our great God and King.

Paul spoke to the Corinthians, reminding them of the weapons of our warfare.

> *For though we walk in the flesh, we do not war after the flesh. For the weapons of our warfare are not carnal but mighty in God for pulling down strongholds, casting down arguments and every high*

thing that exalts itself against the knowledge of God, bringing every thought into captivity to the obedience of Christ and being ready to punish all disobedience when your obedience is fulfilled.

2 Corinthians 10:3-6

In Ephesians 6, we learn in detail of our armor and weapons, but in Paul's word to the Corinthians, he focuses on the purpose of the warfare. He first makes the point, even though we are walking in this life in the flesh or our human body, we are not fighting with human means. He calls human means "carnal." Carnality is simply humankind of reasoning without the benefit of the Holy Spirit's leadership—doing what our minds deem best or reasonable.

The believer has been given weapons from God which are mighty for dealing with the true enemy we are up against. That is Satan and his demonic forces that attack the minds of people and become entrenched in human reasoning and arguments. The verse above clearly teaches us how to activate the weapons of our warfare. Those weapons are prayer and the word of God in the power of the Holy Spirit.

So here it is. We are engaged in the battle for the soul of people. Paul understood that when he preached the word of God, the truth of the good news in Christ, the gospel of the Kingdom of God, that he was pulling down strongholds in the minds of people. He was coming against arguments which the demonic world had created and men believed, especially dealing with idolatry wrapped up in sexual perversion and pleasures of the flesh. All of which was housed in the reasoning of this world's systems.

Paul understood his assignment in warfare—dealing with everything that exalts itself against the knowledge of God. He also understood that he was God's instrument in bringing every thought to the obedience of Christ. He concluded this thought by mentioning the believer's part in the realm of judgment on all disobedience.

This is the context for understanding the necessity of putting on the armor of God and taking up the offensive weapons the Lord has made available to every believer as outlined in Ephesians 6:10-18. It begins with Paul's admonition: "Be strong in the Lord and in the power of His might." It must begin in a relationship with the Godhead through the indwelling of the Holy Spirit who establishes the life of Christ in us. Nothing can happen with any kind of effectiveness without developing our relationship with the Spirit of the Father and the Spirit of the Son which is all contained in the person of the Holy Spirit, the Father's promise to all who believe in Christ (see Luke 24:49 and Acts 1:6-8).

The book of Acts is really the acts of the Holy Spirit through the apostles and those who believed in Christ through their witness. I suggest reading the book of Acts from the perspective of the warfare we have been called to and the armor of God which we are presently studying. This will help in learning to apply what Paul is saying in Ephesians 6:10-18.

Putting on the whole armor is how you enter into verse 10 of Ephesians 6, being strong in the Lord and in the power of His might. You will not be able to stand against the wiles of the devil without the armor of which the Lord has provided for us in Christ. As you put on the armor of God, pray verse 10 as you seek the Lord.

Father, please give me today the strength that comes from you alone. Father, please give me today the power necessary to win the battles that I will encounter. I know that this is what Jesus had in mind when He taught His disciples to pray,

"And do not lead us into temptation, but deliver us from the evil one. For Yours is the kingdom and the power and the glory forever. Amen" (Matthew 6:13).

Ephesians 6:11

*Put on the whole armor of God, that you may be able
to stand against the wiles of the devil.*

The Whole Armor of God

First, it is a decision every individual must make. Deciding to give up your reasoning in exchange for God's reasoning, you have begun the process of becoming equipped (see Proverbs 23:23). His reasoning comes through two standards: 1) the strength of the Word of God and 2) the power of His might which is the Holy Spirit.

It is a recognition that we are in a battle for our lives and the lives of others, not only in the present but also for eternity. It begins with repentance from dead works. Dead works speak of our efforts to live right, to do religion with the hope it pleases God, to keep the rules and believe that it will reward us with heaven. Of course, repentance includes our sin condition both the commission and also omission of sin—a condition that is a nature of sin that is beyond anything we can do about it. It must be acknowledged that our condition is a lost and dying condition. It is a condition of hopelessness. It is a condition of uncertainty concerning our eternal state. Many times, it is a condition that is rooted and grounded in pride. Pride says: *I can take care of myself. I do not need a crutch such as religion. I can pick myself up, thank you very much!* Oh, the strongholds that get a hold on human reasoning through pride. The many arguments against surrendering to God's accepted sacrifice, the Lord Jesus Christ.

Once we surrender to Christ, we receive His victory of overcoming the evil one. That overcoming life is His life now, dwelling in us by the power of the Holy Spirit. As we die to self, that is our sin-nature, we receive His nature rooted in the person of the Holy Spirit.

Before conversion, we were bound by the kingdom of darkness; we just did not know it. Now that the Lord has saved us, delivered us,

164

and given us power to become the children of God, we now enter into His battle to clean up the mess that the devil created in the garden when he tempted Eve and she gave in to the devil's deception. Adam was not an innocent bystander; He knowingly accepted the fruit and joined his wife in disobedience to God's clear command. The enemy took the first round of the warfare with heaven but ended up on his belly. Eventually, the seed of the woman, Jesus, overcame the devil and his kingdom of darkness.

God's plan from the beginning was a people born from heaven's throne by the Spirit of God who would possess the earth. Paul is writing to the Saints of God about their role in the final battle for the nations. This is Satan's last stand. He is already defeated by Christ; he is now going to be defeated by the people of the kingdom so that the nations will be given to the Lord Jesus Christ (see Psalms 2). We are part of this battle and this victory.

It is the wiles of the devil that we are fighting against. It is his trickery. He is a deceiver and a liar from the beginning. Jesus said it this way to the apostate leaders of Israel.

> *You are of your father the devil and the desires of your father you want to do. He was a murderer from the beginning, and does not stand in the truth, because there is no truth in him. When he speaks a lie, he speaks from his own resources, for he is a liar and the father of it.*

John 8:44

The devil tricked Eve and he has been tricking people ever since. He is subtle like a serpent and strikes before you know what struck you. He distorts things so one cannot see clearly to understand what they are up against. He does all this by attacking the thought processes. His target is areas of the soul that are part of one's mind, such as:

- reasoning
- imagination,

- affections
- memory
- conscience

Often, he works through the emotions. As we understand his targets, we can have a better chance of stopping his attacks that come through deception.

As Paul states in verse 11, "Put on the whole armor of God." It will take the whole of the armor of God to defend oneself against the devil. It will take what God supplies. Not psychology, not learned reading, not all the ideas that might cross your mind through collected data. I am not saying those areas are wrong or bad. I'm saying they are not sufficient for the battle we face; not carnal, but mighty through God to pulling down strongholds.

Only the Holy Spirit can supply what is necessary to go up against the devil, the evil one. This is why Jesus taught His disciples to pray: "Lead us not into temptation, but deliver us from evil." Here is the answer to that prayer: "Putting on the whole armor of God."

Notice: this involves standing and not running or hiding. It is not necessarily immediate success, but sometimes it is a long-term battle that we face. I like the old hymn that says:

Standing on the promises of Christ, my King,
Through eternal ages let his praises ring;
Glory in the highest, I will shout and sing,
Standing on the promises of God.
Standing, standing,
Standing on the promises of God, my Savior;
Standing, standing,
I'm standing on the promises of God.

Look at what Paul says about his battles in 2 Corinthians 6:1-10, as I outline it for you:

- We are workers together with Christ.

- "In an acceptable time, I have heard you, and in the day of salvation I have helped you" (Isaiah 49:8).

- Paul says now is the acceptable time, now is the day of salvation. Isaiah was pointing to the Messiah's coming. Paul is saying that God fulfilled His Word in the coming of Christ and in the Helper coming, the Holy Spirit who is in every believer.

- Don't do anything to stumble your brother (see Romans 14:13).

- Be willing to suffer.

Ephesians 6:12

For we do not wrestle against flesh and blood, but against principalities, against powers, against the rulers of the darkness of this age, against spiritual hosts of wickedness in the heavenly places.

The Forces We Fight

The world has no understanding of the spiritual forces which are unseen, but certainly, we see and experience their evil and inside influence on the nations and the people who make up the nations.

For a vivid picture of what Paul is addressing, turn to Daniel 10 where we have one of the clearest pictures of the forces which Paul is describing in Ephesians 6:13. Daniel had received a message from Gabriel in chapter 8 referring to the end of the time of the kings of Media and Persia. Then he speaks of the beginning of the kingdom of Greece. Afterward, he describes the beginning of the Caesars in the Roman Empire.

Daniel 8:25 is interesting, for it states:

> *Through his cunning*
> *He shall cause deceit to prosper under his rule;*
> *And he shall exalt himself in his heart.*
> *He shall destroy many in their prosperity.*
> *He shall even rise against the Prince of princes;*
> *But he shall be broken without human means.*

The *he* in this passage refers to the Caesars and the fall of Rome.

Then in Daniel 9, Gabriel appears again to Daniel and says, "I have come forth to give you skill to understand."

He then prophecies that "Seventy weeks are determined for his people and for the holy city."

That message contained the exact time of Messiah's coming, but in a mystery illustrated by the 70 weeks. Each week represents a period of time according to Ezekiel 4:6 which says: "I have laid on you a day for each year." This is prophetic language that gives us understanding of how to interpret prophetic time periods.

> *Know therefore and understand,*
> *That from the going forth of the command*
> *To restore and build Jerusalem*
> *Until Messiah the Prince,*
> *There shall be seven weeks and sixty-two weeks;*
> *The street shall be built again, and the wall,*
> *Even in troublesome times.*

Daniel 9:25

Understanding the prophetic is a critical component to understanding spiritual warfare because God's enemy, the devil, is at warfare with God's eternal plans and purpose.

In Daniel 10, during the reign of Cyrus king of Persia, Daniel once again fasts and prays for understanding during a time of mourning over Israel's condition and what he received from Gabriel. This time it took three weeks for Gabriel to deliver to Daniel his message from God.

> *And he said to me, "O Daniel, man greatly beloved, understand the words that I speak to you, and stand upright, for I have now been sent to you." While he was speaking this word to me, I stood trembling.*
>
> *Then he said to me, "Do not fear, Daniel, for from the first day that you set your heart to understand, and to humble yourself before your God, your words were heard; and I have come because of your words. But the prince of the kingdom of Persia withstood me twenty-one days; and behold, Michael, one of the chief princes, came to help me, for I had been left alone there with the kings of Persia. Now I have come to*

make you understand what will happen to your people in the latter days, for the vision refers to many days yet to come."

Daniel 10:11-14

Then he said, "Do you know why I have come to you? And now I must return to fight with the prince of Persia; and when I have gone forth, indeed the prince of Greece will come. But I will tell you what is noted in the Scripture of Truth. No one upholds me against these, except Michael your prince.

Daniel 10:20-21

You see beloved, there is a battle going on of which we have little understanding with our natural reasoning.

Gabriel, the messenger archangel, fought with the prince of Persia (the principality over Persia). He needed the help of Michael, the waring archangel, to defeat this principality. After Gabriel completed his mission to deliver God's word to Daniel, he would return, and apparently through Michael, the prince of Persia was defeated. This opened the way for the prince of Greece, who gave power for the Grecian Empire to emerge by defeating Media and Persia.

Even now, in the Middle East, the issue is not Iran, Afghanistan or any other Islamic nation, but principalities and wickedness in high places. It is these enemies that Paul mentions in Ephesians 6:12 that are binding the nations and trying to hold back the gospel of the kingdom. We, like Daniel, must be united in prayer and intercession for the understanding of God's will, for both His people and His will for the nations. Our Father in heaven wants to give to us insight that only can come by the Holy Spirit and a true understanding of the scriptures. In Daniel's day, the plans of God were being revealed and written down as scripture. From the time of the apostles to the present, the will of God is being carried out on the earth through His anointed people.

170

Note that Paul says, "For we...." It is important that we think in terms of members of His body. It is a team effort. Any success that I have had in the gospel of the kingdom has always included others. We cannot be loners in the work of the Kingdom of God.

The battle is a pressure encounter battle. It is indeed like wrestling. By prayer, by the word of God, and by endurance we keep the pressure on the enemy. We strengthen one another by encouragement through love and the keeping of unity of the faith in the bond of peace.

We must always remind ourselves that our warfare is not with flesh and blood. The enemy might work through flesh and blood, but the wrestling is not against flesh and blood but spiritual forces that derive their power from principalities, powers and rulers of the darkness of this age. It is spiritual hosts that are wicked by nature. They reside in heavenly places. They are unseen because they are spirit, but their works are clearly identified by scripture and evidenced in the confusion and havoc they bring upon the human race.

If you want a good read concerning these matters, look up the classic: *The Screwtape Letters* by CS Lewis. He does a great job illustrating the wiles of the devil through a character known as Uncle Screwtape. The devil's assignment for his hordes of demons is to keep a man from coming to Christ. When he fails in that assignment, he focuses on keeping God's people from serving God effectively.

References For Further Study

Principality: *arche* (a)rxh/, NT:746), "beginning, government, rule," is used of supramundane beings who exercise rule, called "principalities"; (a) of holy angels, Eph 3:10, the church in its formation being to them the great expression of "the manifold (or "much-varied") wisdom of God"; Col 1:16; (b) of evil angels, Rom 8:38; Col 2:15, some would put this under (a), but see SPOIL, B, No. 4; (a) and (b) are indicated in Col 2:10. In Eph 1:21, the RV renders it "rule" (KJV, "principality") and in Titus 3:1, "rulers" (KJV,

171

"principalities"). In Jude 6, RV, it signifies, not the first estate of fallen angels (as KJV), but their authoritative power, "their own" indicating that which had been assigned to them by God, which they left, aspiring to prohibited conditions. (from Vine's Expository Dictionary of Biblical Words, Copyright © 1985, Thomas Nelson Publishers.)

Powers: *exousia* (e)cousi/a, NT:1849) denotes "freedom of action, right to act"; used of God, it is absolute, unrestricted, e. g., Luke 12:5 (RV marg., "authority"); in Acts 1:7 "right of disposal" is what is indicated; used of men, authority is delegated. Angelic beings are called "powers" in Eph 3:10 (cf. 1:21); 6:12; 1:16; 2:15 (cf. 2:10). See AUTHORITY, No. 1, see also PRINCIPALITY.

Rulers of the darkness of this age: *kosmokrator* (*kosmokra*/twr, NT:2888) denotes "a ruler of this world" (contrast *pantokrator*, "almighty"). In Greek literature, in Orphic hymns, etc., and in rabbinic writings, it signifies a "ruler" of the whole world, a world lord. In the NT it is used in Eph 6:12, "the world rulers (of this darkness)," RV, KJV, "the rulers (of the darkness) of this world." The context ("not against flesh and blood") shows that no earthly potentates are indicated, but spirit powers, who, under the permissive will of God, and in consequence of human sin, exercise satanic and therefore antagonistic authority over the world in its present condition of spiritual darkness and alienation from God. The suggested rendering "the rulers of this dark world" is ambiguous and not phraseological requisite. Cf. John 12:31; 14:30; 16:11; 2 Cor 4:4.

Spiritual Hosts of Wickedness: *pneumatikos* (*pneumatiko*/$, NT:4152) "always connotes the ideas of invisibility and of power. It does not occur in the Sept. nor in the Gospels; it is in fact an after-Pentecost word. In the NT it is used as follows: (a) the angelic hosts, lower than God but higher in the scale of being than man in his natural state, are 'spiritual hosts,' Eph 6:12; (b) things that have their origin with God, and which, therefore, are in harmony with His character, as His law is, are 'spiritual,' Rom 7:14; (c) 'spiritual' is prefixed to the material type in order to indicate that what the type sets forth, not the type itself, is intended, 1 Cor 10:3,4; (d) the purposes of God revealed in the gospel by the Holy Spirit, 1 Cor 2:13a, and the words in which that revelation is expressed, are 'spiritual,' 13b, matching, or combining, spiritual things with spiritual words [or, alternatively, 'interpreting spiritual things to spiritual men,' see (e) below]; 'spiritual songs' are songs of which the burden is the things revealed by the Spirit, Eph 5:19; Col 3:16; 'spiritual wisdom and understanding' is wisdom in, and understanding of, those things, Col 1:9; (e) men in Christ who walk to please God are 'spiritual,' Gal 6:1; 1 Cor 2:13b [but see (d) above], 15; 3:1; 14:37; (f) the whole company of those who believe in Christ is a 'spiritual house,' 1 Peter 2:5a; (g) the blessings that accrue to regenerate men at this present time are called 'spiritualities,' Rom 15:27; 1 Cor 9:11; 'spiritual blessings,' Eph 1:3; 'spiritual gifts,' Rom 1:11; (h) the activities Godward of regenerate men are 'spiritual sacrifices,' 1 Peter 2:5b; their appointed activities in the churches are also called 'spiritual gifts,' lit., 'spiritualities,' 1 Cor 12:1; 14:1; (i) the resurrection body of the dead in Christ is 'spiritual,' i. e., such as is suited to the heavenly environment, 1 Cor 15:44; (j) all that is produced and maintained among men by the operations of the Spirit of God is 'spiritual,' 1 Cor 15:46.

Ephesians 6:13

Therefore take up the whole armor of God, that you may be able to withstand in the evil day, and having done all, to stand.

Taking Up the Whole Armor of God

We have considered the forces which we are up against: principalities, powers, rulers of the darkness of this present age, spiritual wickedness in the heavenly places. Now we look at the "Therefore" of Ephesians 6:13. Without the armor, which our God has graciously provided, we could not enter into this battle without being utterly destroyed. There is no natural armor or weaponry that can go up against the devil and his demonic realms! Remember Paul's admonition:

For the weapons of our warfare are *not carnal but mighty in God for pulling down strongholds.*

2 Corinthians 10:4

Our weapons are not carnal, that is, not of natural means. But they are mighty through our God for the pulling down of strongholds.

Remember what it says in Ephesians 1:10: "Be strong in the Lord," knowing His word in a daily application and the power of His life, which comes through the Holy Spirit leading us in all that we do. We are never alone, but we are being strengthened always by our Lord Jesus Christ.

You can interpret *we* as referring to "we as individuals," but I believe Paul is addressing *we* as in those who make up an army as His body. It is important to always think in terms of two or three agreeing together, which is the biblical norm. As we consider the army of God, think in terms of a dozen saints making up a platoon that is on a reconnaissance or rescue mission.

One day, as a speaker, I entered a large local church in San Diego. I was addressing a couple of hundred men being trained as disciples of the Lord in the Word of God. The Lord spoke to me and said, "You are not entering a church, but a fortress." He went on to say, "I am raising up my army for the days ahead." A few years later that same church had a very significant move of God. Now, hundreds are being trained and sent out into the San Diego region and to the nations. Many battles are being fought and many victories are being won in the lives of multitudes today. You see, a battle is raging, and only those equipped and sufficiently armed can prevail against the wiles of the evil one.

"Take up the whole armor of God" (Ephesians 6:13). What is the whole armor of God? As we go through what Paul lists here in Ephesians 6, we will detail every aspect of this armor. We also will see that it is not limited to what Paul writes in chapter 6, but he expands upon the armor throughout his epistles.

Now, there is an action you must take. *Pick up.* Let's be practical here. You must pick up your Bible to read it and have the scriptures available to be useful to you. Picking up your Bible is more than reading it. There are other ways to use your Bible in this battle.

To read, meditate, memorize, pray-read the scriptures, and share with others—these are a few ways to "take up the armor." Reading the scriptures is vital to becoming equipped. Read slowly and go back and reread. Cross-reference to other similar passages. It is a good idea to make notes when a scripture leaps out to you as significant. Always meditate upon scriptures that speak loudly to you. Ask the Lord for His insights.

Memorization is important in getting the word into your heart. The Psalmist puts it this way:

> *How can a young man cleanse his way?*
> *By taking heed according to Your word.*
> *With my whole heart I have sought You;*
> *Oh, let me not wander from Your commandments!*

> *Your word I have hidden in my heart,*
> *That I might not sin against You.*

Psalms 119:9-11

Not only is this good counsel for the young man, but aged men and women too!

Prayer-reading the scriptures is another way of getting the word into your inner being and being equipped for the battle. What do I mean by prayer-reading? Pray the word which you are reading back to the Lord. It is His word and His promises. So, our reading back to Him is a wonderful form of praying and reading the scriptures at the same time. That form of praying and reading helps to open our spirit to hear and receive from the Spirit of God.

Whenever the Lord shares an insight with you and brings edification to your spirit and soul, always share that insight with another person, especially a person who is close to you. This helps to establish you in the insight and truth that the Lord is giving. It also allows you to share with another from your relationship with Christ.

I have mentioned a few ways to put on the armor of God. I am sure that the Lord has many ways the Holy Spirit can lead us as it relates to the armor He has given to us as His warring people. Yes, we are solders of His cross. We are sent into the world to represent His kingdom and we know there are many enemies of Christ who are motivated and directed by spiritual forces to resist us. Many times, we are not aware of what we are battling. God wants to make us aware, and give to us His victory over darkness and to manifest His light.

Our purpose of taking up the whole armor of God is so we may be able to withstand in the evil day. Be assured, the enemy has his eyes on you. He has strategized ways to trip you up. If we understand what Paul is instructing God's people to do, we then understand it is preparation for the battles. If we are ready and have the armor on always, we will be prepared "against the wiles of the devil" (v11). I cannot underscore preparedness enough. In fact, this is what the armor is all about. It is our daily walk with Christ in the power of the Holy Spirit. As mentioned in the past, the armor here is not like the clothing we remove when going to bed and then redressing in the morning. Think of it this way: the armor is a lifestyle. It is a spiritual, mental attitude as we will see in each of the parts Paul mentions. Paul uses different illustrations regarding the parts of the armor as he writes in other letters to the churches.

Standing In the Evil Day

Standing in the evil day is part of the instruction. Evil is what we are up against. Satan's kingdom is evil. His evil is worked upon God's creation man. His evil is imparted to man, and his evil is worked through man. Satan is in absolute opposition to God's plan of righteousness, peace, and joy in the Holy Spirit through the sacrifice of God's Righteous One, the Lord Jesus Christ. Remember beloved what we learned as we began our study.

> *In Him we have redemption through His blood, the forgiveness of sins, according to the riches of His grace which He made to abound toward us in all wisdom and prudence, having made known to us the mystery of His will, according to His good pleasure which He purposed in Himself.*

Ephesians 1:7-9

We stand in His good pleasure. Our battles are fought with this stand in mind. We are fully furnished with what we need to prevail. Even in the evil day, we win. Part of the battle for some is suffering in various ways in this life. For others, it is martyrdom, while for others it does not seem so difficult, but we all are waring for the same result— His good pleasure, purposed in Himself so that He is all in all (see Philippians 2:13).

Ephesians 6:14

Stand therefore, having girded your waist with truth,
having put on the breastplate of righteousness,

Truth Holds Everything Together

We have covered the understanding of the verb *to stand*. Paul spoke of standing in the evil day. Evil is what we are up against. Satan's kingdom is evil. His evil is worked upon God's creation man. His evil is imparted to man, and his evil is worked through man. Satan is in absolute opposition to God's plan of righteousness, peace, and joy in the Holy Spirit through the sacrifice of God's righteous one, the Lord Jesus Christ. Remember what we learned as we began our study in Ephesians.

We stand in His purpose. The purpose of Himself! As I said previously, our battles are fought with this in mind. We are fully furnished with what we need to prevail. Even in the evil day, we win. Part of the battle for some is suffering in various ways in this life. I have mentioned a few ways of suffering, the most sacrificial being martyrdom. We all are waring for the same result—His good pleasure, purposed in Himself so that He is all in all.

From the passage above: "having girded your waist with truth." This is also translated as "the belt of truth." It is truth that holds everything together. When I buckle my belt, I think of how important that belt is. For one, it cinches my waist and gives me a sense of security. When the belt is worn properly, I do not need to be adjusting my pants for comfort, to keep them snug or moving from side to side. It is the truth we hang everything else upon.

Jesus said, "I am the way, the truth, and the life. No man comes to the Father except through me" (John 14:6). Jesus spoke this word to His disciples. It was specially directed to Thomas who said in verse 5: "Lord, we do not know where You are going, and how can we know the way." Jesus is that belt of truth. The belt is a person. The belt is a relationship. The belt is knowing in our knower that we can trust Him who has made the Father known to us. And in that knowledge, we know who we are as a son or a daughter. We know who we are as a family member. That is, a member of the family of God.

> *For through Him we both have access by one Spirit to the Father. Now, therefore, you are no longer strangers and foreigners, but fellow citizens with the saints and members of the household of God.*

> Ephesians 2:18-19

Peter gives us help and understanding in what he writes to the saints.

> *But also for this very reason, giving all diligence, add to your faith virtue, to virtue knowledge, to knowledge self-control, to self-control perseverance, to perseverance godliness, to godliness brotherly kindness, and to brotherly kindness love. For if these things are yours and abound, you will be neither barren nor unfruitful in the knowledge of our Lord Jesus Christ. For he who lacks these things is shortsighted, even to blindness, and has forgotten that he was cleansed from his old sins.*

> *Therefore, brethren, be even more diligent to make your call and election sure, for if you do these things you will never stumble; for so an entrance will be supplied to you abundantly into the everlasting kingdom of our Lord and Savior Jesus Christ.*

> *For this reason, I will not be negligent to remind you always of these things, though you know and are established in the present truth. Yes, I think it is right, as long as I am in this tent, to stir you up by reminding you, knowing that shortly I must put off my tent, just as*

our Lord Jesus Christ showed me. Moreover, I will be careful to ensure that you always have a reminder of these things after my decease.

2 Peter 1:5-15

In these verses, Peter exhorts the saints from his life walk what it means to grow and develop in faith, virtue, knowledge, self-control, and more, making one's "call and election sure." Adherence to his instructions will assure "standing and not stumbling." This is our checkpoint to evaluate how well we are wearing the armor of God.

Peter references the trustworthy prophetic word from Matthew 17:5; Mark 9:7; Luke 9:35.

For we did not follow cunningly devised fables when we made known to you the power and coming of our Lord Jesus Christ, but were eyewitnesses of His majesty. For He received from God the Father honor and glory when such a voice came to Him from the Excellent Glory: "This is My beloved Son, in whom I am well pleased." And we heard this voice which came from heaven when we were with Him on the holy mountain.

And so we have the prophetic word confirmed, which you do well to heed as a light that shines in a dark place until the day dawns and the morning star rises in your hearts; knowing this first, that no prophecy of Scripture is of any private interpretation, for prophecy never came by the will of man, but holy men of God spoke as they were moved by the Holy Spirit.

2 Peter 1:16-21

Those holy prophets—men who were sent by God—spoke truth. They gave us a belt that holds everything else together. The Father sent the truth in the person of His Son. Then He spoke from heaven and

180

confirmed Jesus to those disciples. Now, through their faithful and truthful word, we too have this truth in us.

Here is one last point regarding the belt of truth. Peter tells us in 1 Peter 1:13 to "Gird up the loins of your mind." Isn't that interesting that Peter connects loins to our minds? Paul spoke of "girding our waist with truth" (Ephesians 6:14). Paul is using the metaphor of a soldier going into battle. Peter is addressing where the truth must have its effect. This is learning to think the way God thinks and having God-like faith.

Having Put on The Breastplate of Righteousness

When did we put this breastplate on? It was when the righteousness of Christ was given to us through faith. We received His righteousness as we put His righteousness on in exchange for our unrighteousness and dead works. This is why repentance from dead works is the first principle of the doctrine of Christ mentioned in Hebrews 6:1. Faith toward God follows that first principle of Christ.

Imagine taking off your unrighteousness and putting on His righteousness. This piece of spiritual clothing, or in this case, armor, is what has been given to us to wear all the time. It is how we guard our hearts and minds.

Romans 3 gives to us an important explanation of what God has accomplished in Christ regarding this righteousness.

> *But now the righteousness of God apart from the law is revealed, being witnessed by the Law and the Prophets, even the righteousness of God, through faith in Jesus Christ, to all and on all who believe. For there is no difference; for all have sinned and fall short of the glory of God, being justified freely by His grace through the redemption that is in Christ Jesus, whom God set forth as a propitiation by His blood, through faith, to demonstrate His righteousness, because in*

181

His forbearance God had passed over the sins that were previously committed, to demonstrate at the present time His righteousness, that He might be just and the justifier of the one who has faith in Jesus.

Where is boasting then? It is excluded. By what law? Of works? No, but by the law of faith. Therefore we conclude that a man is justified by faith apart from the deeds of the law. Or is He the God of the Jews only? Is He not also the God of the Gentiles? Yes, of the Gentiles also, since there is one God who will justify the circumcised by faith and the uncircumcised through faith. Do we then make void the law through faith? Certainly not! On the contrary, we establish the law.

Romans 3:21-31

Faith in Christ, and the receiving by the faith of what Christ did for us in His redemptive work, comprise the breastplate of righteousness. Once again, we must understand the metaphor being used by Paul. It is not about a piece of clothing that is worn and removed; it is about a lifestyle of righteousness that came from God through faith in God's work in Christ Jesus our Lord!

Ephesians 6:15

And having shod your feet with the preparation of the gospel of peace,

The Good News of Peace

In biblical times it was customary to wash a person's feet when they entered your home after a long dusty walk. It was the result of the walk that cleansing was needed. The walk which God has called us to is a walk of the good news of peace. The road can be rough and often there are lots of problems along the way. Rejection is not an uncommon experience. Regardless, we are to walk out the peace of God. That is, not just talk about it but demonstrate peace in our nature and attitude even toward the unlovely and the God deniers.

For me, some of my earliest lessons came when I was in the California Army National Guard. Basic training in 1967 was my first experience away from family and my mostly Christian friends. My first week of basic training was challenging to say the least, as I heard foul language, dirty stories, and male ego trying to find its place and acceptance among other men. I met and came under Army Sergeants, called DI's, exerting absolute authority. Nothing was a suggestion. My options were to do it or suffer the consequences.

That week, I prayed this prayer: "Father, how can I live for you in this place?" The Lord's answer was simple very simple, "Be you." For me, that meant reading my Bible regularly. It meant don't be phony or something you are not. Live as a son of God. Don't be a moralist. Don't be judgmental or condemning, but be peaceful and loving in all you do and say. He helped me to be prepared for rejection, but He also gave me great favor with my peers and superiors. There are so many stories I could talk about concerning the road that the feet shod with the gospel of peace walks upon.

Covering And Protection

This part of the armor of God provides a covering and protection for the feet. The feet speak of our daily walk. I am reminded of what David the Psalmist said in Psalm 18.

> *He makes my feet like the feet of deer,*
> *And sets me on my high places.*
> *He teaches my hands to make war,*
> *So that my arms can bend a bow of bronze.*
> *You have also given me the shield of Your salvation;*
> *Your right hand has held me up,*
> *Your gentleness has made me great.*
> *You enlarged my path under me,*
> *So my feet did not slip.*

Psalm 18:33-36

The rest of the psalm is a very worthwhile read. It is the testimony of King David and the warfare he faced. It is a picture of "having done, all to stand." David testifies how the Lord armed him with strength for the battle and how his enemies fell under his feet. Below are other psalms which David wrote along with the sons of Korah.

> *My eyes are ever toward the Lord,*
> *For He shall pluck my feet out of the net.*

Psalm 25:15

> *And have not shut me up into the hand of the enemy; You have set my feet in a wide place.*

Psalm 31:8

> *He also brought me up out of a horrible pit,*
> *Out of the miry clay,*
> *And set my feet upon a rock,*
> *And established my steps.*

Psalm 40:2

He will subdue the peoples under us,
And the nations under our feet.

Psalm 47:3

For You have delivered my soul from death.
Have You not kept my feet from falling,
That I may walk before God
In the light of the living?

Psalm 56:13

Who keeps our soul among the living
And does not allow our feet to be moved.

Psalm 66:9

Solomon writes:

Ponder the path of your feet,
And let all your ways be established.
Do not turn to the right or the left;
Remove your foot from evil.

Proverbs 4:26-27

How beautiful upon the mountains
Are the feet of him who brings good news,
Who proclaims peace,
Who brings glad tidings of good things,
Who proclaims salvation,
Who says to Zion,
"Your God reigns!"

Isaiah 52:7

What a great biblical study to be had concerning the feet. I have to move on, but you could camp on the subject of your feet and your walk before the Lord for a long time!

Preparation Of the Walk

Preparation is a very important word. Previously I mentioned my beginning time in the Army. That beginning was about preparation for going into combat for our country. Little did I know, it was also a time when God prepared me for the battles I would face in life and the spiritual warfare ahead. Preparation and our walk are vital to understanding if we want to please the Lord and experience His favor in all we do.

What is meant by preparation? It is the same as preparing for a successful trip. Preparation is the first step toward success. Knowing where, when, how, and the necessary luggage needed, what do I do when I arrive? Who will I be with and who will I meet?

We are ordained to carry good news to everyone in our sphere. The good news is that God's anger has been satisfied, His demand of righteousness has been met. We are to offer people peace with God, peace in their minds, peace with others, a community of peace, a peace that comes out of righteousness and delivers joy unspeakable and full of glory. Listen to what Peter says in his first epistle.

> *But sanctify the Lord God in your hearts, and always be ready to give a defense to everyone who asks you a reason for the hope that is in you, with meekness and fear; having a good conscience, that when they defame you as evildoers, those who revile your good conduct in Christ may be ashamed.*

> 1 Peter 3:15-16

Peter learned well from Jesus who had this to say recorded in Matthew 20:28:

> *For even the Son of Man came not to be served but to serve others and to give his life as a ransom for many.*

Our feet carry us on a journey of serving others and that translates to giving our life for them, maybe not as Jesus in dying for the sins of all mankind, but in simply living our lives for the benefit of others. Listen to Paul's counsel in Romans 12:

> *Let love be without hypocrisy. Abhor what is evil. Cling to what is good. Be kindly affectionate to one another with brotherly love, in honor giving preference to one another, not lagging in diligence, fervent in spirit, serving the Lord; rejoicing in hope, patient in tribulation, continuing steadfastly in prayer; distributing to the needs of the saints, given to hospitality. Bless those who curse you; bless and do not curse. Rejoice with those who rejoice, and weep with those who weep. Be of the same mind toward one another. Do not set your mind on high things, but associate with the humble. Do not be wise in your own opinion. Repay no one evil for evil. Have regard for good things in the sight of all men. If possible, as much as depends on you, live peaceably with all men.*

Romans 12:9-18

In our study of Ephesians 6:15, and having shod your feet with the preparation of the gospel of peace, we have looked at a comprehensive view of this part of the armor of God. The armor is a lifestyle of Christ in us, the hope of glory.

Ephesians 6:16

*Above all, taking the shield of faith with which you will
be able to quench all the fiery darts of the wicked one.*

Above All

Having studied Ephesians 6:15: "And having shod your feet with
the preparation of the gospel of peace," we now move to "Above all."
Why is the shield of faith put into the context "Above all"?

The writer of Hebrews makes this powerful statement in Hebrews
11:6.

> *But without faith it is impossible to please Him, for he
> that comes to God must believe that He is, and that He
> is a rewarder of those who diligently seek Him.*

Do you believe this? The writer of Hebrews did. He was seeking
to establish these Hebrew Christians in their faith which was under
attack as evidenced by what he said to them in chapter 6. Paul takes up
the same reasoning in Galatians as he seeks to protect the Galatian
Gentile Christian community who were being deceived by men who
were distorting the gospel of peace and disrupting the faith of the
Gentile believers. Listen to what Paul said to these believers.

> *O foolish Galatians! Who has bewitched you that you
> should not obey the truth, before whose eyes Jesus
> Christ was clearly portrayed among you as crucified.*

Galatians 3:1

Paul is using strong language because of the seriousness of their
error. Many in the Christian faith have also been bewitched through
another gospel, which is not the good news we have in Christ. That
error is to think that through some work or good that we do, we will
obtain favor with God. The truth is, there is nothing you and I can do,
apart from faith in Christ Himself, to receive God's favor as a means

of righteousness that is imputed through faith. The bent of a human is to try and work our way right with God. That is a spiritual bewitching, a deception of the evil one to stumble us.

Consider Ephesians 6:11: "Put on the whole armor of God that you may be able to stand against the wiles of the devil." So here is another aspect of standing, that of standing in God's righteousness alone. Paul goes on to say to the Galatian believers:

> *This only I want to learn from you: Did you receive the Spirit by the works of the law, or by the hearing of faith?" Are you so foolish? Having begun in the Spirit, are you now being made perfect by the flesh?*

> Galatians 3:2-3

I am sorry to report that many of God's people are in the same place as were these Galatian believers. Beginning by faith alone, but then believing they need to do something to earn God's favor. Only by faith can we defeat the evil one. This is faith centered in what the Lord Jesus completely accomplished, fully satisfying the wrath of God toward sin, then receiving God's gift, His promised Holy Spirit, which seals His promises to us (see Ephesians 1:13).

Can you see with me that taking the shield of faith happened when we received Christ? You are protected from the lie of the enemy which says: *You are not good enough, you have not done enough, and you cannot receive from God because you do not meet up to the requirements. The enemy wants us to just keep trying. Just one more thing and you will attain.*

No! Don't be bewitched. Jesus Christ is the only sufficient one. Exercise faith in His full and completed work. When the enemy lies to you, just declare your faith in Christ's finished work. "Jesus did it all, all to Him I owe. Sin had left a crimson stain, but He washed it white as snow!" There is nothing more I can do! Do not be bewitched by lies. This is what James means when he says:

> *Therefore submit to God. Resist the devil and he will flee from you.*

> James 4:7

We are speaking of a lifestyle regarding the Armor of God. The shield of faith is just that—a life lived by the faith of the Son of God (see Galatians 2:20). This applies in all things, in every action we take, and should be part of every plan we make. We live rooted and grounded in Christ because of His finished work. That finished work includes our spirit, our soul, and our body.

> *Now may the God of peace Himself sanctify you completely; and may your whole spirit, soul, and body be preserved blameless at the coming of our Lord Jesus Christ. He who calls you is faithful, who also will do it.*

> 1 Thessalonians 5:23-24

Paul begins his point with the mention of peace. Remember verse 15: "Feet shod with the preparation of the gospel of peace." He is the God of peace. May He Himself sanctify you! Only Christ can do this. Only through the power of the Holy Spirit can we be sanctified or set apart for God's will. Stop working at it and simply yield to His gentle help. Begin to worship from your spirit. Tell Him of Your desperate need and desire for His presence. Ask Him for new levels of faith to be granted to you so you can receive all He has to give to you. This is allowing your spirit to be prepared to receive what He desires to give you. Always thank Him for His faithfulness and His kindness toward you.

I love how Peter brings things together in this regard in his first epistle:

> *Therefore gird up the loins of your mind, be sober, and rest your hope fully upon the grace that is to be brought to you at the revelation of Jesus Christ; as*

obedient children, not conforming yourselves to the former lusts, as in your ignorance; but as He who called you is holy, you also be holy in all your conduct, because it is written, "Be holy, for I am holy."

1 Peter 1:13-16

Sanctified Warfare

Our warfare is fought in the context of His Holiness! It is sanctified warfare!

And if you call on the Father, who without partiality judges according to each one's work, conduct yourselves throughout the time of your stay here in fear; knowing that you were not redeemed with corruptible things, like silver or gold, from your aimless conduct received by tradition from your fathers, but with the precious blood of Christ, as of a lamb without blemish and without spot. He indeed was foreordained before the foundation of the world, but was manifest in these last times for you who through Him believe in God, who raised Him from the dead and gave Him glory, so that your faith and hope are in God.

1 Peter 1:17-21

We are to walk in the fear of the Lord. We are to live our lives in the fear of God, not afraid, but with reverence and godly fear. Our redemption is precious, but not like silver and gold, but by the precious blood of Jesus we have been redeemed. All this was predetermined before the foundation of the world. But it is now manifested in these last times. The last times was not the end of the world two thousand years ago. It was the end of the Adamic effort to please God. It was the end of the law as a means of righteousness. It was the beginning of a whole new creation in the Holy Spirit (see 2 Corinthians 5:17) which supports what Peter is saying in the verses quoted above.

The Enduring Word

Since you have purified your souls in obeying the truth through the Spirit in sincere love of the brethren, love one another fervently with a pure heart, having been born again, not of corruptible seed but incorruptible, through the word of God which lives and abides forever, because

"All flesh is as grass,
And all the glory of man as the flower of the grass.
The grass withers,
And its flower falls away,
But the word of the Lord endures forever."

Now this is the word which by the gospel was preached to you.

1 Peter 1:22-25

The Holy Spirit is where regeneration begins in the seed of the Word of God; it is where the believer begins their journey of sanctification.

Having been born again, not of corruptible seed but incorruptible, through the word of God which lives and abides forever.

1 Peter 1:23

Through Jesus' work on the cross, he brought the old creation to an end. It is a new day in the Spirit. God raised Jesus from the dead and gave Him glory. Our faith and hope are in God. In that hope we fight the good fight of faith to be part of bringing into the earth heaven's kingdom and heaven's will. And here is where it begins.

Since you have purified your souls in obeying the truth through the Spirit in sincere love of the brethren, love one another fervently with a pure heart.

1 Peter 1:22

This is a perfect definition of the sanctification of the soul. It is the practical, daily walk that expresses itself in love.

Lastly, Paul mentions the sanctification of our bodies. The body is strongly affected by the natural senses. Those senses are directly taking in the natural aspects of life as well as the result of sin and its fleshly manifestations. Only by the sanctifying work of the Holy Spirit can we keep ourselves pure from the impurities of this world's systems. This takes faith that originates in the faith of the Son of God.

The shield of faith is a shield that protects these three areas of our lives: the spirit, the soul, and the body. All three have been saved by the redemptive work of Christ. Faith for eternal life begins in our spirit. That faith begins to grow in us through God's Word and the work of the Holy Spirit. That faith begins to affect how we think and act. That work is a result of faith in our souls. It is through this faith that we learn and are empowered to bring our flesh under the lordship of Christ in this present world. At the same time, we look ahead to the world that is coming.

I hope you have a better understanding of why Paul said of the shield of faith: "Above all, taking the shield of faith" (Ephesians 6:16). Faith is necessary for every aspect of our walk with God. The last element Paul mentions in this verse is, "Quench all the fiery darts of the wicked one." Those darts are aimed at every area of our walk with Christ.

The darts take on many different forms. It could be in the form of distractions so we do not spend devotional time with our Lord. Consider the darts of busyness, materialism or entertainment. Or the darts of emotional stress, manifested in worry, anxiety and fretting.

There are the darts of financial debt manifested in unfaithfulness in our giving such as tithing, offerings and ministering to the poor.

Consider the dart of health issues that have curable root causes such as wrong eating habits, poor sleeping habits, and a lack of discipline in exercise. There are many other darts I could mention. Seek the Lord for His understanding of what darts the enemy might be throwing at you. Seek the Lord for an impartation of faith to deal with the enemy's attacks on your life. Many times, the connecting of our faith with the faith of others to whom we are joined is what is needed to quench the fiery darts of the wicked one.

Ephesians 6:17

And take the helmet of salvation, and the sword of the Spirit, which is the word of God;

The Helmet of Salvation

Notice the phrase: "take the helmet." Paul said the same thing previously in verse 13: "take up" the whole armor of God. Then again in verse 16: "taking up" the shield of faith. As I said previously, Christ has done it all, so then our faith is exercised in what Christ has accomplished. Yet, there is an action on our part. That action is manifested in faith or receiving what Christ has done, received through our obedience by faith. The taking up is an act of obedience to the Lord's finished work. Our authority is derived from Christ Himself who said, "All authority has been given to Me in heaven and on earth. Go therefore and make disciples of all nations" (Matthew 28:18-19). It begins with His faith and obedience and is worked out through our faith and obedience to Jesus.

So what does it mean to "take the helmet of salvation"? In the past, I have taught on the threefold salvation our Lord has given to us. 1 Thessalonians 5:23 gives a picture for our spirit, soul, and body relating to our threefold salvation by sanctification or being set apart unto God. Even though salvation is a gift from God, we must fight to protect that gift. The wicked one is always trying to take our salvation from us in terms of how we see God and how we see His love and provision for us. The helmet represents the battle for our minds, which includes our reasoning, affections, imaginations, conscience, and memory.

Let's consider the battle going on for each one of these areas of our mind. We begin with our reasoning. Have you ever heard it said, "God helps those who help themselves?" Some think this is a scripture reference, but it's not. The Bible says just the opposite. Repentance has to do with changing your mind about *how* you think.

How do we reason? Is it by the world's standards or by God's standard—His eternal word? This is the battleground where we battle. Is our reasoning based upon the prism of man's authority or God's eternal word? What we must settle is this area of authority. Is it rooted in man or is it rooted in what God declares—His eternal Word?

> *All scripture is given by inspiration of God, and is profitable for doctrine, for reproof, for correction, for righteousness, that the man of God may be equipped for every good work.*

2 Timothy 3:16-17

Next, let's consider our affections. Paul writes saying:

> *If then you were raised with Christ, seek those things which are above, where Christ is, sitting at the right hand of God. Set your mind on things above, not on things on the earth. For you died, and your life is hidden with Christ in God.*

Colossians 3:1-3

This is what Paul means when he says: "Have the mind of Christ." All Jesus did was in direct obedience to His Father in heaven (see John 5:19, 1 Corinthians 2:16, and Philippians 2:5-8).

Many of our battles are directly connected to where our affections lie or what consumes our minds. The question each of us should be asking is this: "Is what I think and what I love directly connected with obedience to God's word?" Are my thoughts and actions aligned with the word of God, and do they bring glory to Him?

These questions lead us to the next area of consideration regarding the helmet of salvation. One of the great needs of our mind is redeemed imaginations. The realm of imagination is the creative center of one mind. An unredeemed imagination is centered on oneself. Religion and religious works are a product of man's imaginations. *What can I do to appease God? I will do this or that and He will be happy with me and accept me.* The reality is there is nothing we can do to please God in our work and strength. As we have seen, only faith alone centered on the completed work of Christ can satisfy God's will and plan. That is why religion binds multitudes of people all over the world. Jesus has saved us from vain imaginations and given us a new mind to receive what God has planned, which is for us to join Him in His work of redemption for mankind. This is an important part of the helmet of salvation we are instructed to take and put on.

Part of our battle is to go after vain imaginations. Vain imaginations are where strongholds attach themselves and become that which controls one's life. Paul brings focus when he says:

> *For the weapons of our warfare are not carnal but mighty in God for pulling down strongholds, casting down arguments and every high thing that exalts itself against the knowledge of God, bringing every thought into captivity to the obedience of Christ,*

> 2 Corinthians 10:4-5

Paul makes clear his assignment as an apostle of Christ's, but it also teaches us that each believer is engaged in a battle for the thoughts and imaginations—the strongholds rooted in the mind.

Consider how the helmet of salvation relates to the conscience.

> *How much more shall the blood of Christ, who through the eternal Spirit offered Himself without spot to God, cleanse your conscience from dead works to serve the living God?*

> Hebrews 9:14

> *Let us draw near with a true heart in full assurance of faith, having our hearts sprinkled from an evil conscience and our bodies washed with pure water.*

> Hebrews 10:22

It is the conscience that affects our sense of need to work our way right with God. But those works are dead works because nothing could satisfy our sin condition except the blood of Jesus Christ. When our conscience is cleansed, we can draw near with a true heart. We can come with full assurance of faith because our evil conscience and even our bodies are washed with pure water. It's pure because of what it speaks to in Christ: His death, burial, and resurrection. This is the only acceptable sacrifice.

> *Pray for us; for we are confident that we have a good conscience, in all things desiring to live honorably.*

> Hebrews 13:18

Our conscience needs to be clear toward all men and before God. The conscience becomes the clearinghouse regarding our motives. It is being able to look a person straight in the eye and say, "All I have done toward you, I have done with a good conscience before God."

Lastly, let's consider our memory. The memory, both conscious and subconscious, needs cleansing from hurts, offenses, and sin that opened doors to the enemy to have a legal right in one's life. This is a vast subject that we cannot cover here. I will say this: many come to Christ but never deal with the past in depth. They struggle to forgive and be able to forget because of hurts, offenses, and the sin which is still locked up in their memory.

Forgiveness from the heart is vital to a healthy Christian lifestyle. Matthew 18 records the parable of the unforgiving servant. Understanding what Jesus is teaching here is critical to understanding the helmet of salvation. Many of God's people are struggling with deep issues that involve them forgiving from the heart. Paul understood the importance of a good conscience when he said in Acts 24:16: "I myself always strive to have a conscience without offense toward God and men." As we work out our salvation, we must make sure we have laid hold of the helmet. Make sure that it is fitted in place.

The Sword of The Spirit

*And take the helmet of salvation, and the sword of the
Spirit, which is the word of God.*

The metaphor of a sword is a great choice for an illustration of
what the Word of God does when handled skillfully by a son or
daughter of God.

*The word of God is living and powerful, and sharper
than any two-edged sword, piercing even to the
division of soul and spirit, and of joints and marrow,
and is a discerner of the thoughts and intents of the
heart. And there is no creature hidden from His sight,
but all things are naked and open to the eyes of Him to
whom we must give account.*

Hebrews 4:12-13

Ephesians 6:17 instructs us to take the sword of the Spirit. The
book of Hebrews speaks of that sword as two-edged. The sword of the
Spirit first is wheeled to deal with our own heart condition. By the
Word of God, we can discern every thought and intent of our own
hearts. We ask: do my thoughts and intentions align with God's
thoughts and intentions? How could I know, except by the teaching of
God's Word? Through the discipline of memorizing and meditating on
God's word, His word becomes established in my heart.

An illustration from the book of Proverbs helps us understand how
God's word can be used to discern our hearts. Look at Proverbs 11:1,
the biblical teaching of scales or balances. "Dishonest scales are an
abomination to the Lord, but a just weight is His delight." Is our heart
right when it comes to commerce? Do we do business with this
principle in mind?

Verse 2: "When pride comes, then comes shame; but with the
humble is wisdom." Do we think of ourselves first or another, thereby
maintaining an attitude of humility?

Verse 3: "The integrity of the upright will guide them, but the perversity of the unfaithful will destroy them." Is there integrity in all I do?

Verse 4: "Riches do not profit in the day of wrath, but righteousness delivers from death." Is righteousness the foundation of all our motivations? Where does money fit into our value system?

So, we see how the Word of God is the sword of the Spirit in dealing with one's own heart. Now we turn our thinking toward the sword of the Spirit in dealing with the hearts of others. We have used 2 Corinthians 10:3-5 before, but it is powerful to make our point here.

> *Though we walk in the flesh, we do not war after the flesh. For the weapons of our warfare are not carnal but mighty in God for pulling down strongholds, casting down arguments and every high thing that exalts itself against the knowledge God, bringing every thought into captivity to the obedience of Christ"*

> 2 Corinthians 10:3-5

How is this done? It is done by the sword of the Spirit which is the word of God. Consider Paul as he preached, taught, and debated God's Word. In Acts 17, Paul and his team preached and taught in Thessalonica by reasoning with the Jews from the scriptures. They did this for three Sabbaths. Some of the Greek proselytes were persuaded, but the Jews were not. This caused a great division in Thessalonica. Many times, the scriptures divide by cutting through unbelief and establishing the true believers.

It was different in Berea. They received the word with all readiness and searched the scriptures daily to find out whether these things were so. Later in Acts 17, Paul and his team share with some of the philosophers of his day, on Mars Hill in Athens Greece, as recorded in Acts 17:29-34. There were three responses to Paul's preaching the resurrection from the dead: the mockers, those who wanted to hear more, and those who believed the word of God.

The word of God can be viewed three ways:

1. A written word—the *grapho*.

2. A living word—the *logos*.

3. A spoken word—the *rhema*.

Grapho Speaks of the Written Word of God

All Scripture is given by inspiration of God, and is profitable for doctrine, for reproof, for correction, for instruction in righteousness.

2 Timothy 3:16

Holy men of God were moved by the Holy Spirit.

Knowing this first, that no prophecy of the Scripture is of any private interpretation." For prophecy never came by the will of man, but holy men of God spoke as they were moved by the Holy Spirit.

2 Peter 1:20-21

The completed canon of scripture is God's written word to the whole world. At Vision International University, our motto is "Taking the Whole Word to the Whole World."

The Logos

The phrase "the word of the Lord," i.e., the revealed will of God, is used very frequently in the Old Testament. It is used of a direct revelation given by Christ (see 1 Thessalonians 4:15); of the gospel (See Acts 8:25; 13:49; 15:35,36; 16:32; 19:10; 1 Thessalonians 1:8; 2 Thessalonians 3:1). In this respect, it is the message from the Lord, delivered with His authority and made effective by His power (see Acts

10:36). Jesus Himself said, "I am the way, the truth, and the life. No one comes to the Father except through Me" (John 14:6). Jesus is the *logos*!

The Rhema

Personal word: *rhema* (NT:4487) denotes "that which is spoken, what is uttered in speech or writing"; in the singular, "a word."

The significance of *rhema* (as distinct from logos) is exemplified in the injunction to take "the sword of the Spirit, which is the word of God" (Ephesians 6:17). Here the reference is not to the whole Bible as such, but to the individual scripture which the Spirit brings to our remembrance for use in time of need, a prerequisite being the regular storing of scripture in the memory. Remember how we dealt with the memory. Not only can we be healed of hurtful past memories, but we can be fortified with a memory; filled with God's goodness as revealed in His Eternal Word, the sword of the Spirit.

The Prophetic Side of the Sword of The Spirit

He had in His right hand seven stars, out of His mouth went a sharp two-edged sword, and His countenance was like the sun shining in its strength.

Revelation 1:16

The Sharp Two-Edged Sword

As we read further in Revelation 1, the seven stars mentioned in verse 12 are revealed as the angels of the seven churches. And the seven lampstands are revealed as the seven churches in verse 20. That study is for another time. For right now, let's focus on the sharp two-edged sword coming out of His mouth. In Revelation 19:10 we discover that "the testimony of Jesus is the spirit of prophecy." The word of God is prophetic.

God spoke to Adam and Eve that her seed would crush the head of the serpent. There are over 800 scriptures in the Old Testament that speak of Jesus coming and of His kingdom that He would establish here on earth. Prophesy's that speak of the time of His birth, the place of His birth, being rejected by His people, His death, His burial, and His resurrection. There is prophecy speaking of the coming of the Holy Spirit, the redeemed people of Israel and the adding of the Gentiles and so much more. It is a very large sword that is coming out of His mouth. That sword cuts the captives free, but also brings judgment to those who reject His word.

In Revelation 2-3, the sword represents Christ's word to the seven churches to repent or suffer judgment. That sword honored the faithful believers but warned the unfaithful members of the body. It also represented the judgment soon to happen to Israel and Jerusalem, in fact, judgment on the whole Jewish system. Judgment because they rejected God's Anointed one who now reigns from heaven. All this was what Jesus spoke in Matthew 24 and was now soon to come to pass.

Consider Revelation 2:12-16 which speaks to the compromising church at Pergamos. "And to the angel of the church in Pergamos write, These things says He who has the sharp two-edged sword: I know your works, and where you dwell, where Satan's throne is. And you hold fast to My name and did not deny My faith even in the days in which Antipas was My faithful martyr, who was killed among you, where Satan dwells. But I have a few things against you because you have there those who hold the doctrine of Balaam, who taught Balak to put a stumbling block before the children of Israel, to eat things sacrificed to idols, and to commit sexual immorality. Thus, you also have those who hold the doctrine of the Nicolaitans, which things I hate. Repent, or else I will come to you quickly and will fight against them with the sword of My mouth.

Briefly: Nicolaitans were one of the heretical sects that plagued the churches as men who "lead lives of unrestrained indulgence." They are related to Gnostics and Gnosticism. John, the disciple of the Lord, preaches the faith concerning (the deity of Christ), He seeks, by the proclamation of the Gospel, to remove that error. Error was brought by Cerinthus which had been disseminated among men, and a long time previously by those termed Nicolaitans. John's message was that he might confound them, and persuade them that there is but one God, who made all things by His Word.

The doctrine of the Nicolaitans appears to have been a form of antinomianism, which makes the fatal mistake that man can freely partake in sin because the Law of God is no longer binding. It held the truth on the gratuitous reckoning of righteousness; but supposed that a mere intellectual "belief" in this truth had a saving power (See Theopedia).

This doctrine continued into the Second Century and even is found in the thinking of many today that identify with the Christian Church. What Christ did in His death on the cross and in the power of his resurrection was to free us from the "Law" as a means of righteousness." He is our righteousness by faith in His completed work of redemption. From the righteousness of Christ, the believer is freed from the power of sin to live out the righteousness of Christ presently through the power of the Holy Spirit freely given from the Father.

One last point is that the Nicolaitans believed in the error of "domination" over God's people. This belief produced a "hierarchy" of domination rather than "servant leadership" which Christ established in His apostolic ministry and seen in His apostle's ministry and the foundation they laid.

The Sword that Judges

Now I saw heaven opened, and behold, a white horse. And He who sat on him was called Faithful and True, and in righteousness, He judges and makes war. His eyes were like a flame of fire, and on His heads were many crowns. He had a name written that no one knew except Himself. He was clothed with a robe dipped in blood, and His name is called the Word of God. And the Armies in heaven, clothed in fine linen, white and clean, followed Him on white horses. Now out of His mouth goes a sharp sword, that with it He should strike the nations. And He Himself will rule them with a rod of iron. He Himself treads the winepress of the fierceness and wrath of Almighty God. And He has on His robe and on His thigh a name written: KING OF KINGS AND LORD OF LORDS.

Revelation 19:11-16

Notice that Paul says in Ephesians 6:17: "The sword of the Spirit." It is the Spirit of the Lord in us which gives life to the word of God that comes through us as we speak God's Word to others.

And take the helmet of salvation, and the sword of the Spirit, which is the word of God; praying always with all prayer and supplication in the Spirit, being watchful to this end with all perseverance and supplication for all saints.

Ephesians 6:17-18

We have considered the metaphor of a sword for the word of God. We saw that the Word of God is living and powerful, and sharper than any two-edged sword, piercing even to the division of soul and spirit, and joints and marrow, and is a discerner of the thoughts and intents of the heart.

We learned that we are to take the sword of the Spirit and use it to first discern our own heart, and then use it to deal with the hearts of others—the heart of their minds where imaginations and arguments against God are fortified by the enemy through the systems of the world. We also learned we can discern every thought and intent of our own heart, by asking, do my thoughts and my intent align with God's thoughts and intents. How could I know, except by the teaching of

God's Word? Through the discipline of study, memorizing, and meditating on God's word, His word becomes established in my heart.

We learned of three expressions of scripture (the word of God). They are:

1. The *grapho* (written word of God or recorded word).
2. The *logos* (the revealed word of God).
3. The *rhema* (the personal word of God).

Lastly, we discover that the word of God is prophetic:

> *And I fell at his feet to worship him. But he said to me, "See that you do not do that! I am your fellow servant, and of your brethren who have the testimony of Jesus. Worship God! For the testimony of Jesus is the spirit of prophecy."*

> Revelation 19:10

Remember, this is the prophetic side of the "Sword of the Spirit. Do not try to figure this out through natural means, such as your natural reasoning or interpretation of scripture. Remember, it is the Sword of the Spirit! It is only the Holy Spirit that can bring true revelation of the prophetic.

The world faces this same word of judgment today. As God judged the holy nation in the first century, as God judged the churches down through the ages, and as God judged Rome, He is presently pouring out His Spirit on the church and in the world offering salvation to those who will believe. The Lord is also getting ready to judge the world's system that has rejected His Anointed King.

There were many things John the Baptist could have said about Jesus, but the bottom line was that Jesus Christ would baptize with the Holy Spirit and fire. Think of it, friends. The whole world is going to be baptized by Jesus, either by the Holy Spirit, who will baptize us into Christ, or with the fire of judgment, which is the righteous result of the governmental prayers and prophetic decrees of the Lord's apostles and saints (see Matthew 16:19, Acts 2:16-20, Revelation 8:3-5 and 18:20).

Verses 17 and 18: Part of taking the helmet of salvation and the sword of the Spirit, which is the word of God and the next admonition, is praying always with all prayer and supplication in the Spirit, being watchful to this end with all perseverance and supplication for all saints.

"Pray without ceasing" (1 Thessalonians 5:17). In this passage, Paul joins together several admonitions in his encouragement to the Thessalonica believers: rejoice always, pray without ceasing, in everything give thanks, God's will, do not quench the Spirit, don't despise prophecies, test everything and then hold fast to what is good, abstain from all evil (see 1 Thessalonians 5:16-21).

Next, Paul joins together prayer and supplication. Although it is a noun, supplication comes from the Latin verb *supplicare*, which means "to plead humbly." It is used 60 times in the Bible. While a supplication is often thought of as a religious prayer, it can logically be applied to any situation in which you must entreat someone in power for help or a favor.

Most people regard both as terms describing prayers with no difference between them. Supplication is a form of prayer but considered as kneeling and bending down in which someone makes a humble petition or an entreaty to God. Prayer, however, can be defined as sincere thanksgiving or requests made to God.

Paul is not speaking about formal religious prayer, but a humble petition by the unction of the Holy Spirit that is Spirit-led prayer. This can include what Paul describes as praying in the spirit when he says,

> *Therefore let him who speaks in a tongue pray that he may interpret, for if I pray in a tongue, my spirit prays, but my understanding is unfruitful. What is the conclusion then? I will pray with the spirit, and I will*

pray with the understanding. I will sing with the spirit, and I will also sing with the understanding.

1 Corinthians 14:13-15

Prayer also includes being watchful. *Watchful* means "perseverance and supplication for all saints." What we see once again in Ephesians is a lifestyle—a lifestyle of prayer, a lifestyle of gratitude, and a lifestyle of watching and evaluating what is happening through the prisms of the Word of God.

One of the most significant changes that take place when we truly become a kingdom man or woman is our concern for other saints. No longer is the focus me, myself, and I. Nor is it just my household. It is all saints. Practically speaking, this means all those within my sphere of influence, but also those who are leaders within our city, state, and nation. Most importantly is praying for the persecuted church, praying for all those sent out on a mission to the nations. In other words, as Paul said, *all saints*.

Can you see how the armor of God is coming together and how important it is to each believer as Soldiers of the Cross of Jesus?

Ephesians 6:18

Praying always with all prayer and supplication in the Spirit watchful to this end with all perseverance and supplication for all saints…

Pray Always

Verse 17 spoke about the helmet of salvation and the sword of the Spirit, how they are connected to prayer and supplication in the Spirit. Now consider how verses 18 through 20 are inter-related, that is, prayer for all saints and specific prayer for Paul.

What Paul is instructing concerning prayer, for many, is unimaginable and quite a difficult discipline. These verses can be easily skipped over, right? How can one pray always? Let's see…

First, we must rid ourselves of religious ideas of prayer. To name a few: going to a building to pray. Prayer is not a position like kneeling or closing your eyes. Kneeling and closing one's eyes can be part of our prayer practice, but not essential to prayer itself!

Prayer is first and most importantly a lifestyle. When the disciples asked Jesus to teach them to pray, He was not teaching them a recited prayer but the components of prayer. Think about what Jesus taught concerning prayer.

In this manner, therefore, pray:

> *Our Father in heaven,*
> *Hallowed be Your name.*
> *Your kingdom come.*
> *Your will be done*
> *On earth as it is in heaven.*
> *Give us this day our daily bread.*
> *And forgive us our debts,*
> *As we forgive our debtors.*
> *And do not lead us into temptation,*

But deliver us from the evil one.
For Yours is the kingdom and the power
And the glory forever. Amen.

Matthew 6:9-13

- *Our Father* – prayer is fundamental to our relationship with God who is our Father. He is the Father of our Lord Jesus Christ who makes it possible through the work of the Holy Spirit to give to each believer regeneration or being born again. We are regenerated or born again by the Holy Spirit's power working in us. As a new creation in Christ, (see 2 Corinthians 5:17), we have a longing to spend time with our heavenly Father in prayer and His word.

- *Which art in heaven* – A clear distinction is made between a natural father and our Heavenly Father. God is the Father of a new creation man and woman. We have seen this throughout the book of Ephesians. One New Man in Christ. He is the head and we are His body. He is our High Priest. We are a kingdom of Priests.

- *Hollowed be your name* – Our God, who is our Father, is altogether holy. Only by prayer and the word of God can one begin to perceive how holy is our great God and Father. In His presence, His glory moves on us and is in us to move through us. It is from His presence we can enter into true worship as Jesus said in John 4:23-24.

But the hour is coming, and now is, when the true worshipers will worship the Father in spirit and truth; for the Father is seeking such to worship Him. God is Spirit, and those who worship Him must worship in spirit and in truth.

- *Your kingdom come. Your will be done on earth as in heaven* – The message is the kingdom. To be sure, the message is not the church. The church (the body of Christ) is the messenger and not the message. This is a crucial mistake that has been made down through history, beginning in the second century. The twentieth and twenty-first centuries are about bringing the church back to her primary message—the kingdom of God. This was Christ's message and this was the apostle's message: *Repent! For the kingdom of God is at hand.* That kingdom came in the person of the Holy Spirit (see Romans 14:17). Christ is reigning today over the kingdom of darkness and the nations. It is our responsibility to permit Him to reign in us, His people, and proclaim His reign to the nations.

- *Your will be done* – God's will was first established and done by Jesus, His only begotten Son. God's will is that the Lord's church would declare His will to the nations. God's purpose is that the life of Jesus is revealed in and through the body of Christ on the earth even as in heaven (see Hebrews 12:18-29). This is why unity or the understanding, of the one new man, is so vital.

- *On earth as it is in heaven* – This passage reveals the great connection between heaven and earth. The Holy Spirit has been given from heaven and the Lord continues to pour out His Spirit as He gives an unshakable kingdom to His sons and daughters.

- *Give us today our daily bread* – Remember what Jesus told the Devil: "Man shall not live by bread alone, but by every word that proceeds from the mouth of God" (Matthew 4:4). God is our source of natural sustenance. "My God shall supply all your need according to His riches in glory by Christ Jesus" (Philippians 4:19). What we desperately need is the sustaining Word of God, the *rhema* or personal daily bread of life.

- *Forgive us our debts as we forgive our debtors.* – Here is a key to a successful life in Christ—receiving the absolute forgiveness of God because of the absolute completeness of what Christ Jesus did for mankind. It is so complete that it is as far as the east is from the west that He has removed our sins from us. He expects us to forgive in the same way as He forgives us. Our ability to do just that comes from the power and grace of the Holy Spirit of Christ in us. It is not by your work of righteousness, but His work of righteousness in you. The classic scripture is found in Matthew 18 in the parable of the unforgiving servant.

- *And do not lead us into temptation; But deliver us from the evil one.* – One of the roles of the Holy Spirit in our lives is to lead away from temptation.

> *No temptation has overtaken you except such as is common to man; but God is faithful, who will not allow you to be tempted beyond what you are able, but with the temptation will make a way of escape, that you may be able to bear it.*

1 Corinthians 10:13

This passage does not remove our responsibility in dealing with temptation. Listen to what James writes.

> *Let no one say when he is tempted, "I am tempted by God"; for God cannot be tempted by evil, nor does He Himself tempt anyone. But each one is tempted when he is drawn away by his own desires and enticed. Then, when desire has conceived, it gives birth to sin; and sin, when it is full-grown, brings forth death.*

James 1:13-15

Peter writes in 1 Peter 5:8-11:

> *Be sober, be vigilant; because your adversary the devil walks about like a roaring lion, seeking whom he may devour. Resist him, steadfast in the faith, knowing that the same sufferings are experienced by your*

212

brotherhood in the world. But may the God of all grace, who called us to His eternal glory by Christ Jesus, after you have suffered a while, perfect, establish, strengthen, and settle you. To Him be the glory and the dominion forever and ever. Amen.

- *For yours is the kingdom and the power and the glory forever* – The foundation is the kingdom of God. The kingdom is speaking about the government of God. I am speaking about His right to rule all things. It is His Kingdom which we are receiving. His kingdom is in power. It is the power of the Holy Spirit. Not just healing and miracles, but the power to raise the dead.

Even when we were dead in trespasses, made us alive together with Christ (by grace you have been saved), and raised us up together, and made us sit together in the heavenly places in Christ Jesus.

Ephesians 2:5-6

Beloved, you and I speak of the glory of God. Paul, in writing to the Colossians, reveals that this is a mystery.

The mystery which has been hidden from ages and from generations, but now has been revealed to His saints. To them God willed to make known what are the riches of the glory of this mystery among the Gentiles; which is Christ in you, the hope of glory.

Colossians 1:26-27

It is prayer made with supplication–that is, prayer made in humility and prayer that is led by the Spirit of God. As the disciples of old asked Jesus to teach them to pray, we also need the help of the Holy Spirit to lead us in our priestly service to the Lord. Spirit led prayer! Being filled with the Holy Spirit will result in praying Spirit led prayers at all times.

Ephesians 6:19-20

And for me, that utterance may be given to me that I may open my mouth boldly to make known the mystery of the gospel, for which I am an ambassador in chains; that in it I may speak boldly, as I ought to speak.

Apostolic Stewardship

The apostolic function is a stewardship trust. All the apostles were given the responsibility to be true to the Word of God which the Lord Jesus gave them from the Father (see John 17:11-17). Those apostles were not given the luxury of holding to their own opinions but were given a stewardship to know and teach the mysteries of the kingdom of God.

Jesus told His disciples that He would give to them "the keys of the kingdom." Those keys were hidden in mystery in the Old Testament. Only by revelation did they become understood. The apostles, including Paul, understood what they carried and knew they were responsible to communicate the keys of the kingdom, which is the understanding of the mysteries of the kingdom. They understood that the message of the kingdom was for both the Jews and Gentile nations. Thus, as Jesus commands, "Go therefore and make disciples of all the nations" (Matthew 28:19). This is what Paul was asking for. As a steward of the mysteries of God, he was praying that he might speak boldly.

Let a man so consider us, as servants of Christ and stewards of the mysteries of God. Moreover, it is required in stewards that one be found faithful.

1 Corinthians 4:1-2

In the scripture above, Paul speaks of being a servant of Christ. That is what a steward is—a servant trusted with what belongs to His master. The mysteries of the kingdom of God belong to Jesus our Lord

214

and our Savior. Note, this is not Jewish doctrine; this is not some denomination's doctrine. The mysteries are Christ's doctrine given to Him by the Father and established through His resurrected life.

> *Truly, these times of ignorance God overlooked, but*
> *now commands all men everywhere to repent, because*
> *He has appointed a day on which to judge the world*
> *in righteousness by the Man whom He has ordained.*
> *He has given assurance of this to all by raising Him*
> *from the dead*

Acts 17:30-31

Paul understood his call and responsibility given to him by the Lord. He is asking those who received the message of the kingdom and the understanding of the mysteries to stand with him through prayer regarding the task of preaching this word of the Lord with boldness. *Boldness* because it is risky when the gospel is accurately preached. Why? Because it is aimed at all men everywhere, including, emperors, kings, governors, dictators, and presidents. Most apostles were martyred because of their challenges.

Mystery Of Christ

I want to speak to the mystery of Christ. We will be looking at the mysteries of the Kingdom of God. These are the mysteries given to the apostles of our Lord for His New Testament church that we might understand what Christ has accomplished in the Father's will. I will name the mysteries of which Paul was speaking. All of these mysteries need serious study, but I will simply mention them here.

- Mystery of Godliness

> *And without controversy great is the mystery of godliness:*
> *God was manifested in the flesh,*
> *Justified in the Spirit,*
> *Seen by angels,*

Preached among the Gentiles,
Believed on in the world,
Received up to glory.

1 Timothy 3:16

- Mystery of His will

Having made known to us the mystery of His will,
according to His good pleasure which He purposed in
Himself, that in the dispensation of times He might
gather together in one all things in Christ, both which
are in heaven and which are on earth—in Him.

Ephesians 1:9-10

And to make all see what is the fellowship of the mystery,
which from the beginning of the ages has been hidden in
God who created all things through Jesus Christ.

Ephesians 3:9

Paul, in Galatians 4:4, called this, "The fullness of the time." The
new creation in Christ began 2,000 years ago. It is not a future event
but is in the process even as we speak. It will calumniate in Christ
return and the judgment of the nations as mentioned in Acts 17:31.

- Mystery of the Indwelling Christ: The ministry and
  stewardship Jesus gave to Paul.

Of which I became a minister according to the
stewardship from God which was given to me for you,
to fulfill the word of God, the mystery which has been
hidden from ages and from generations, but now has
been revealed to His saints. To them God willed to
make known what are the riches of the glory of this
mystery among the Gentiles: which is Christ in you,
the hope of glory.

Colossians 1:25-27

216

- Mystery of Iniquity or Lawlessness: "For the mystery of lawlessness is already at work" (2 Thessalonians 2:7). This is what the believer is up against. The antidote is the mystery of the resurrection. Christ raised and seated above all principalities, all powers, the rulers of the darkness of this age, and against spiritual hosts of wickedness in heavenly places (see 2 Thessalonians 2:3-8).

- Mystery of Christ and His Church

  For we are members of His body, of His flesh and of His bones. "For this reason a man shall leave his father and mother and be joined to his wife, and the two shall become one flesh." This is a great mystery, but I speak concerning Christ and the church.

  Ephesians 5:30-32

- Espoused to Christ presently (see 2 Corinthians 11:2).

- In Spirit joined now (see 1 Corinthian 6:17).

- Our bodies are on earth, He is up in Heaven (see 2 Corinthians 5:6-8).

- A Mystery that can't be explained. We are to believe this reality by faith as we walk in the Spirit.

  This is a great mystery, but I speak concerning Christ and the church.

  Ephesian 5:32

- The Mystery of the restoration of Israel

  For I do not desire, brethren, that you should be ignorant of this mystery, lest you should be wise in your own opinion, that blindness in part has happened to Israel until the fullness of the Gentiles has come in.

  Romans 11:25

The first 40 years was the Jewish mission (first the Jew then the Gentile). Paul always went to the Jew first. Judgment upon Israel, the system, came in 70 AD. Jews were scattered among the Gentile nations. A great gathering back into their geographical land has taken place in our day. A Jewish State has been established among the nations. This mystery is in the fact that God has established His true Israel through the cross of Christ. The true Israelite is found in the Spirit. Born from Jerusalem above (Galatians 4:26), circumcised of the heart (Romans 2:29), and not under the written law, but the Law of the Spirit of Life in Christ Jesus (Romans 8:1-2). The some-total of the mystery is found in Galatians 3:25-29. The true Israel of God is in heaven, also the true Mount Zion, the heavenly Jerusalem (Hebrews 12:22-29).

Many Jews of the flesh will be born again and added to the true Israel of God that has been regenerated by the Spirit. They are part of the harvest of the nations before the coming of Christ in judgment of all the nations who have rejected Him as sovereign king.

• Mystery Babylon

> *And on her forehead a name was written:*
> *MYSTERY, BABYLON THE GREAT,*
> *THE MOTHER OF HARLOTS*
> *AND OF THE ABOMINATIONS*
> *OF THE EARTH.*

> Revelation 17:5

This was God's charge against Jerusalem and the Jewish apostate system which crucified their Messiah under Roman rule and authority. It is the same charge against Jerusalem that is found in the Old Covenant. According to Jeremiah 3:8, God divorced her under the Old Covenant. In the new Covenant, He redeemed her through the blood of Christ, which is all those who believed and trusted Christ, receiving the promised Holy Spirit. Those of Israel who did not trust in Christ, He destroyed in 70 AD, fulfilling His word spoken in Matthew 21-25.

- Mystery of Change

"We will not all sleep, but we all shall be changed."

Behold, I tell you a mystery: We shall not all sleep, but we shall all be changed—in a moment, in the twinkling of an eye, at the last trumpet. For the trumpet will sound, and the dead will be raised incorruptible, and we shall be changed. For this corruptible must put on incorruption, and this mortal must put on immortality. So when this corruptible has put on incorruption, and this mortal has put on immortality, then shall be brought to pass the saying that is written: "Death is swallowed up in victory."

> *"O Death, where is your sting?*
> *O Hades, where is your victory?"*

1 Corinthians 15:51-55

Ephesians 6:21-24

But that you also may know my affairs and how I am doing, Tychicus, a beloved brother and faithful minister in the Lord, will make all things known to you; whom I have sent to you for this very purpose, that you may know our affairs, and that he may comfort your hearts. Peace to the brethren, and love with faith, from God the Father and the Lord Jesus Christ. Grace be with all those who love our Lord Jesus Christ in sincerity. Amen.

Serving

Tychicus is mentioned several times in the New Testament.

- Acts 20:4 - Part of Paul's apostolic team

- Colossians 4:7 - Sent to Colossi to tell the saints of Paul's welfare

- 2 Timothy 4:12 - Sent to Ephesus

- Titus 3:12 - possibly sent to get Titus

Paul was diligent in keeping the saints aware of his status. Communication is vital in the body of Christ. God's leaders need to keep the saints informed so that they know how to pray and stay in close partnership with the Lord's apostolic government.

Notice Paul's emphasis on "beloved brother, faithful minister." There are many ways to serve the King's house. One way for Tychicus was as an entrusted member of Paul's apostolic company. He served the fellowship of the apostles. That fellowship was concerning the apostolic mandate each of the apostles carried. The mandate to declare that God's Messiah King is installed and reigning presently from heaven.

Tychicus was sent to make known Paul's affairs and to comfort the hearts of the people regarding Paul's sufferings.

As Paul closes his letter, he does so with a familiar valediction: "Peace." His message of love with faith is a direct blessing from God the Father and the Lord Jesus Christ. He speaks as their representative. Paul's standard greeting and salutation is about God's grace on those who love our Lord Jesus Christ in sincerity.

Amen.

Overview of Ephesians

Chapter 1

"He chose us in Him before the foundation of the world" (v1). This is the bedrock of the entire epistle, but also the bedrock of our entire salvation. We learned that God has made known to us "the mystery of His will, according to His good pleasure which He purposes in Himself, hat in the dispensation of the fullness of times He might gather together in one all things in Christ, both which are in heaven and which are on earth—in Him" (v9-10).

The apostolic prayer for all ages is found in verse 17: "That the God of our Lord Jesus Christ, the Father of glory, may give to you the spirit of wisdom and revelation in the knowledge of Him."

The finished work in Christ is recorded in verse 22.

> *And He put all things under His feet, and gave Him to be head over all things to the church, which is His body, the fullness of Him who fills all in all.*

Chapter 2

Those who have trusted in Christ have been "made alive, who were dead in trespasses and sins" (v1). He made us alive together in heavenly places in Christ Jesus—a present reality to be revealed in the ages to come.

The Gentiles that were without hope and alien to the commonwealth of Israel, strangers from the covenants of promise, having no hope and without God in the world, now in Christ Jesus have been brought near by the blood of Christ (see verses 12-13).

We have seen how the blood of Jesus reconciled both the Jew and the Gentile to God in one body through the cross, thereby putting to death the enmity giving each access by one Spirit to the Father.

God's household is now built upon the foundation of the apostles and the prophets, Jesus Christ Himself being the chief cornerstone, in which the whole building is being fitted together, grows into a holy temple in the Lord.

Chapter 3

Paul clarifies the mystery he was given. He calls it the mystery of Christ. That the Gentiles should be fellow heirs of the same body and partakers of His promise in Christ through the gospel.

Again, Paul calls this, "The unsearchable riches of Christ" (v8). Paul calls it, "The fellowship of the mystery" (v9).

> *Now to Him who is able to do exceedingly abundantly above all that we ask or think, according to the power that works in us.*

> Ephesians 3:20

Chapter 4

The focus is on Christ's ascension and the bestowing of gifts from Christ to His church. The fivefold ministry gifts are the ministry graces of Christ Himself.

The objective of Ephesians 4 is about growing up into Christ, becoming a mature person and a mature body resulting in the unity of the faith and the knowledge of the Son of God, to a perfect man, the measure of the fullness of Christ.

The consistent encouragement of Paul is the putting off, concerning our former conduct, the old man which grows corrupt according to deceitful lusts. We are to put on the new man which was created according to God, in true righteousness and holiness (v22-23).

224

And do not grieve the Holy Spirit of God, by whom you were sealed for the day of redemption.

Ephesians 4:30

Chapter 5

Here Paul instructs us in purity, the contrast between darkness and light. That we are not to have any, "Fellowship with the unfruitful works of darkness, but rather expose them" (v11).

In this chapter, Paul gave instructions for family order beginning with wife and husband. Paul connects the marriage relationship as a picture of Christ and His church. Paul speaks to this as, "A great mystery, but I speak concerning Christ and His church" (v32).

Chapter 6

Paul speaks of children in the Christian family, then he deals with masters and bondservants.

From there, Paul opens up our understanding of the spiritual warfare in which we are engaged. He speaks to putting on the whole armor of God, that our battle is not with flesh and blood but with principalities, powers, against the rulers of the darkness of this age, against spiritual hosts of wickedness in the heavenly places.

The armor is pictured as how a Roman soldier would be readied for battle. Paul ends with bringing together the battle array and prayer warfare.

We learn of the importance of:

Praying always with all prayer and supplication in the Spirit, being watchful to this end with all perseverance and supplication for all the saints—and for me, that utterance may be given to me, that I may open my mouth boldly to make known the mystery of the gospel, for which I am an ambassador in chains; that in it I may speak boldly, as I ought to speak.

Ephesians 6:18-20

Finally, we learn of the apostolic stewardship of the mysteries of the gospel of the Kingdom of God.

About the Author

George Runyan gave his life to Christ in 1958. He received his calling from the Lord in 1960. He was ordained in 1973. He holds a BA in Theological Studies, a Master of Theological Studies (MTS), and an Honorary Doctorate of Divinity (DD).

George has been involved with planting twelve congregations both nationally and internationally. He is Founder and Director of City Church Ministries, networking with hundreds of pastors and civic leaders throughout the San Diego region. He is a Faculty member of Vision International University where he serves on the Board of Regents. George started the San Diego Healing Rooms and helped to establish the East County Healing Center in El Cajon, CA. He is an author and has been a radio broadcaster for many years.

George is working with ministers from other cities who carry a similar vision for a united church in the locality. His passion is to see the walls of separation between churches, ethnic groups and civil government broken down. He has a strong apostolic teaching and counseling anointing.

George has authored several booklets, training materials, and has two books on the Person and Work of the Holy Spirit, one on Spiritual Warfare, and a Commentary on the Book of Ephesians. He has a business background, having begun two successful electronic businesses. This has provided many opportunities in the marketplace for both consulting and sharing biblical principles to develop kingdom-based businesses. It also provides the opportunity for "marketplace evangelism." He serves on several 501 (c) 3 non-profit boards.

George and his lovely wife, Becky, have eight children and nineteen grandchildren. They live near San Diego, California.

Other Resources Available From George Runyan

MANDATED, Promise of Greater Works Fulfilled

ISBN: 1-59352-213-4

A DAILY DEVOTIONAL, Developing Your Relationship with the Holy Spirit

ISBN: 978-1-61529-052-9

FIT FOR ENGAGEMENT, A Spiritual Warfare Manual

ISBN: 978-1-61529-213-4

SALVATION TRUTHS – God's Salvation Plan for His Threefold Creation Man

HIGHWAY to HEALING – A God Given Ministry

CONCERNING SPIRITUAL GIFTS STUDY

LAYING FOUNDATIONS MANUAL

RECOMMENDED RESOURCES

www.csmpublishing.org

www.foothillschurch.org

www.ftfmin.org

www.rejoiceministriesinternational.com

www.signofthekingdom.com

www.booksbyvision.org

Notes

Ephesians 1

Notes

Ephesians 2

Notes

Ephesians 3

Notes

Ephesians 4

Notes

Ephesians 5

Notes

Ephesians 6